THE POLITICAL WRITINGS
OF JAMES HARRINGTON

D0291136

The Library of Liberal Arts
OSKAR PIEST, FOUNDER

. . . .

The Library of Liberal Arts

THE POLITICAL
WRITINGS OF
JAMES
HARRINGTON

Representative Selections

Edited, with an introduction, by
CHARLES BLITZER
American Council of Learned Societies

· ·

The Library of Liberal Arts
published by

THE **BOBBS-MERRILL** COMPANY, INC.
A SUBSIDIARY OF HOWARD W. SAMS & CO., INC.
Publishers • INDIANAPOLIS • NEW YORK

James Harrington: 1611-1677

· · · · · · · · · · · · · · · · · · ·

PREFACE

The choice of the pieces included in this volume was a relatively simple matter. Given the aim of the volume—to present in a limited space the most complete and accurate picture of James Harrington's political thought—the choice was almost automatic. Harrington's Introduction to his *Commonwealth of Oceana,* which contains the fullest exposition of the fundamentals of his system, was indispensable. Since Harrington's reputation and influence have rested chiefly upon his theory of the political importance of property and of the property-owning classes, it seemed highly desirable to include those portions of the *Oceana* that are most relevant to this subject, passages which have the added advantage of giving something of the flavor of that unusual work. A slight problem was raised by the necessity of dealing briefly with the complex institutional proposals that form the heart of the *Oceana,* covering scores of detailed and rather tedious pages. Fortunately, this was a problem that Harrington himself had faced three centuries ago; in order to make his proposals more presentable to his contemporaries, he wrote a brief abstract of the institutions of his "equal commonwealth," entitled *The Rota,* which exactly meets our needs. Finally, the conciseness and clarity of Harrington's last, posthumously published work, *A System of Politics Delineated in Short and Easy Aphorisms,* made it ideal for a collection such as this.

Once these selections had been made, the problem of arrangement also proved to be quite simple. Since all of Harrington's political writings were produced in the five years from 1656 to 1660, and since his ideas developed not at all during this period, it was unnecessary to be bound by any strictly chronological order. Indeed, it seemed best to ignore chronology completely and to begin with *A System of Politics . . . ,* which serves as an excellent introduction to Harrington's system, being at the same time short, comprehensive, and eminently readable. After *A System of Politics,* I have chosen to follow Harrington's own pattern, beginning with his discussion of the fundamentals of politics, going on to the more specific treatment of the questions of property and aristocracy, and concluding with an outline of the institutional structure that he put forward as the concrete embodiment of his political theory.

I might add that this collection represents less an attempt to popularize Harrington than an attempt to make available, once more, the most important of his writings. Thus, I have not been particularly concerned to avoid completely the painfully detailed discussions and the almost endless citations of authority that have helped to create Harrington's reputation as an unreadable author. To have done so would, I believe, have seriously distorted the true character of Harrington's writings and destroyed most of the value of this collection. The reader who finds himself wearied by these details and citations may find some comfort in remembering that a consistently racy and entertaining Harrington would, after all, not be Harrington.

Spelling, punctuation, capitalization, and editorial style have been revised to conform to current American usage. Obvious typographical errors have been corrected.

Finally, I should like to express my deep gratitude to three scholars who have generously helped me in the preparation of this volume: Carl J. Friedrich, of Harvard University, under whose kind and expert guidance I first undertook the study of James Harrington's political thought; Cecil Driver, of Yale University, who tried (with scant success, I fear) to give my prose style something of the grace and elegance that distinguish his own; and Harry Hubbell, of Yale, whose erudition made the identification of even the most obscure classical passages seem easy.

C. B.

CONTENTS

· · · · · · · · · · · · · · · · ·

THE POLITICAL WRITINGS
OF JAMES HARRINGTON

Part One
A SYSTEM OF POLITICS

Part Two
THE COMMONWEALTH OF OCEANA

Part Three
THE ROTA

CHRONOLOGY

1603 James VI of Scotland comes to the English throne as James I.

1611 January 3, birth of James Harrington.

1618 Beginning of the Thirty Years' War.

1620 Arrival of Pilgrims at Plymouth; publication of Bacon's *Novum Organum*.

1621 The Great Protestation of the Commons of England.

1625 Accession of Charles I.

1628 The Petition of Right; assassination of Buckingham.

1629 Harrington enters Trinity College, Oxford; beginning of eleven years of "personal rule" of Charles I.

c. 1631–c. 1635 Harrington's travels on the continent.

1639 Beginning of the first Bishops' War; Harrington travels to Scotland with Charles I.

1640 November 3, beginning of the Long Parliament (to March 16, 1660).

1642 Beginning of the First Civil War.

1644 Milton's *Areopagitica*.

1645 Harrington submits petition on behalf of Elector Palatine.

1646 End of the First Civil War.

1647 Charles I surrendered to parliament; Harrington is appointed Groom of the Bedchamber, accompanies king to the Isle of Wight.

1648 The Second Civil War.

1649 January 30, execution of Charles I; beginning of Harrington's temporary retirement. Establishment of the Commonwealth.

1651 Publication of Thomas Hobbes' *Leviathan*.

1653 Dissolution of the Rump; establishment of the Protectorate under the Instrument of Government; Cromwell becomes Lord Protector.

1656 Publication of *The Commonwealth of Oceana*.

1657 The Humble Petition and Advice; publication of Matthew Wren's *Considerations on Mr. Harrington's Commonwealth of Oceana* (August 14); publication of Harrington's *Prerogative of Popular Government* (November).

1658 Publication of Harrington's *Stumbling-Block of Disobedience* (February); second edition of *Oceana;* translations from Virgil; *Seven Models of a Commonwealth* (November). Death of Oliver Cromwell (September 3).

1659 The most active year of Harrington's career. Publication of *Pour enclouer le canon* (May 2); *A Discourse upon this saying* . . . (May 16); *The Art of Lawgiving* (June); presentation to parliament of the Harringtonian "Humble Petition of Divers well affected persons" (July 6); *A Discourse Shewing* . . . (July 21); *Politicaster* and *Political Aphorisms* (August); *A Parallel of the Spirit of the People* and *Valerius and Publicola* (October); the Rota Club officially founded.

1660 Publication of Harrington's last pamphlets; final meeting of the Rota Club (February); restoration of the monarchy, Charles II.

1661 December 28, Harrington is committed to the Tower of London; writing of the posthumously published *System of Politics*. End of Harrington's career.

1677 September 7, death of Harrington.

INTRODUCTION

I

In a sense it is ironic that this Introduction should be necessary. Two hundred years ago one would hardly have presumed to "introduce" the political theory of James Harrington to an educated American audience. At the time of the American Revolution, just a century after their author's death, Harrington's writings, which had already exercised a profound influence on the governments of the proprietary colonies of Carolina, New Jersey, and Pennsylvania during the seventeenth century, reached the peak of their popularity in this country, and Harrington himself enjoyed among American political theorists and practitioners a reputation second only to that of John Locke. James Otis was happy to acknowledge his debt to the "divine writings" of "the incomparable Harrington." John Adams, who was at once the most ardent and the most distinguished American disciple of the English theorist, believed that Harrington had discovered "as infallible a maxim in politics as that action and reaction are equal is in mechanics" [1]—a discovery which the second President of the United States considered the greatest since the invention of printing. An earlier president of Yale College, Ezra Stiles, in a famous sermon preached at Hartford in 1783, could think of no higher praise for the governments of New England than that they had "realized the capital ideas of Harrington's *Oceana*." Dr. Stiles perhaps recalled the moment during the Massachusetts constitutional convention of 1779 when a motion was made and seconded to the effect "that the word 'Massachusetts' be expunged [from the new Frame of Government] and that the word 'Oceana' be substituted." Although one suspects that the motion was inspired rather by irony than by admiration of Harrington's theories, its very formulation gives striking proof of the currency of Harrington's ideas and the extent

[1] John Adams to James Sullivan, May 26, 1776. *The Works of John Adams*, ed., Charles Francis Adams (Boston, 1850-1856), IX, 376.

of their influence on the legislators of New England. Nor should it be supposed that Harrington's reputation was confined to a small group of intellectuals—politicians, lawyers, clergymen, and the like. On the contrary, there is evidence that strongly suggests that by the time of the Revolution his name had become almost a household word in the colonies, a popular symbol of the rational defense of liberty against tyrannical pretensions. Thus, in April of 1776, an orator speaking at the grave of General Joseph Warren, the hero of the Battle of Bunker Hill, could assume that the assembled throng would understand his allusion, when he said of his subject: "Like Harrington he wrote—like Cicero he spoke—like Hampden he lived—like Wolfe he died!"

It seems hardly necessary to labor the point that Harrington's fame has diminished considerably during the last two hundred years. This is not the place to enter into a discussion of the reasons for his decline from celebrity in the eighteenth century to near-oblivion in the twentieth; nor is it our intention either to lament his fate, or to condemn it as unjust. What must concern us here is simply the fact that, at some time in the past, in England and France as in America, Harrington was widely thought to deserve a place among the great political theorists of the modern world; when Lord Acton placed his name at the head of "the little band of true theorists," he was expressing a not uncommon opinion of Harrington's worth. As a result, although his name is now virtually forgotten, Harrington's political ideas and his concrete political proposals have in a very real sense become part of our own political heritage. Thus, if one wishes to discover the original *rationale* of many of the characteristic features of the government of the United States—such, for instance, as the written constitution, the secret ballot, the rotation of membership in the Senate—one must look not to *The Federalist* or to the other writings of our Founding Fathers, but rather to Harrington's *Commonwealth of Oceana*. Again, in somewhat more general terms, one cannot hope to understand the genesis or development of the modern theory of the relation between political and economic power, or the modern tradition of civil liberty and liberty of conscience, or the modern doctrine of checks and balances, without consulting Harrington's works. This does not mean, of course, that any of these ideas was completely original with Harrington. On the contrary, the sources of each of them may be found in classical and medieval political theory and practice. Nevertheless, it is unquestionably true that the currency of these institutions and ideas is, in varying degrees, due to Harrington's intercession. Indeed, it may be argued that the obscurity into which Harrington has fallen is a product of the fact that so many of his ideas have been so thoroughly assimilated into our political tradition as to seem mere truisms. But it may also be argued that the most practically significant theorists, and in the long run the most successful, are precisely those whose ideas come to have a life of their own, independent of the reputation of their authors and accepted on all sides as nothing more than statements of what has always been known to be true.

The contemporary reader, coming to Harrington for the first time, cannot fail to be struck by the way in which his writings combine the archaic and the familiar. Despite a style that exhibits much of the turgidity of baroque prose and little of its grandeur, and despite a method of argumentation and "proof" that is clearly old-fashioned, the reader will experience repeated shocks of recognition as he comes upon passages that can only be described as "modern." To say this is not to imply that Harrington's works should be approached as a fascinating storehouse of anachronisms. On the contrary, the crucial point is that, in spite of his flashes of modernity, in spite of his juxtaposition of the old and the new, Harrington created a theory that stands as an integrated whole and as a product both of his age and of his intellectual milieu. Thus, for example, his theory of the economic basis of political power, although based on suggestions in Aristotle, arose directly from his study of history and from his observation of the English constitutional crisis of the seventeenth century. Similarly, his scheme of rotation in office (which still governs elections to the United States Senate), while modeled after a medieval Venetian institution, grew out of Harrington's observation of the English Long Parliament. Thus, more than anything else, Harrington's writings may be said to stand as an impressive testimonial to the continuity of our political tradition.

What has just been said should serve to indicate the basis of our belief that, in order to understand Harrington's ideas and their place in the history of political thought, it is necessary, first, to know at least the bare outline of his life; and, second, to know something of the intellectual tradition in which he worked. Our purpose in what follows is simply to provide this necessary introductory material before allowing Harrington to speak for himself.

II

James Harrington, the oldest son of Sir Sapcotes Harrington and his first wife, the former Jane Samuel, was born at his mother's home in Northamptonshire on January 3, 1611 [1612] —the year of the King James Bible and of *The Tempest*. In the seventeenth century, as indeed throughout most of history, lineage was of crucial importance in determining one's position in society. To say this is to imply, not that it was impossible to rise to great eminence from relatively humble origins, but rather that the path which an individual followed and the careers that were open to him were, to a large extent, ordained by the circumstances of his birth. In this respect James Harrington was exceptionally well-favored. His family, although past its peak by the time of his birth, was still among the most eminent and well-connected in England and until quite recently it had also been among the most prosperous. The Harringtons had settled at Exton in Rutlandshire, England's smallest county, at some time in the twelfth century, and Exton House remained the family seat until its sale in 1613 [1614]. When, in 1684, James Wright came to compile his *History and Antiquities of the County of Rutland,* he felt it necessary to devote almost twice as much space to the Harringtons as to any other family. The high point of the family's fortunes had come at about the time of the accession of Elizabeth, in the middle of the sixteenth century, when a stunning succession of marriages allied the Harringtons with many of the great noble families of England and with at least one Continental royal house. As might be expected, this enhancement of the Harringtons' social position coincided with a marked improvement in their financial status. By the year 1600, Sir John Harrington of Exton, the political theorist's great-uncle, was described as "able to dispend yearly betwixt £5000 and £7000 of good land," an income equal to that of "the best barons"—and, indeed, Sir John was soon to become Baron Harrington and to be appointed governor to the king's daughter, Elizabeth. It is notable that the "rise" of the Harringtons occurred at almost precisely the time chosen by James Harrington as the great turning point of English social history—the period between the reigns of Henry VII and James I (1457-1603), during which, he argued, the "balance of property" in England shifted from the nobility and the clergy to the gentry. Regardless of whether one accepts the theorist's reading of English history and thus attributes his family's rise to the dissolution of the great estates of the nobility and the confiscation of church lands, it is a matter of record that by the end of the seventeenth century the descendants of his great-grandfather included among their number eight dukes, three marquises, seventy earls [sic], nine counts, twenty-seven viscounts, and thirty-six barons.[2] Although James Harrington

---

[2] The list was compiled by Wright in his *History and Antiquities of the County of Rutland* (1684), p. 52. See also the recently published study, *The Gentry 1540-1640*, by H. R. Trevor-Roper (Cambridge, England, 1953), pp. 22-24, for an account of the rise of the Harringtons. Trevor-Roper goes on to detail the decline of the family's fortunes after 1600, but (despite Trevor-Roper's contrary view) this seems hardly relevant to Harrington's theory of the rise of the gentry prior to 1603. I see no reason to reject Tawney's statement that "the process from which [Harrington] generalized had been taking place beneath his eyes. His own relatives had been engaged in it."

received no honor from the rulers of England and is therefore
not included in this distinguished catalogue, he did enjoy
during his lifetime the considerable advantages of gentle
birth. Notably, he received an excellent education; he was
able to associate easily with the greatest and most highly
placed personages of his age; and, as the first of his father's
four sons, he never faced the necessity of earning a living. In
short, Harrington clearly belonged to that aristocracy which
he was to describe as possessing "nothing else but their education and their leisure for the public, furnished by their ease
and competent riches, and their intrinsic value." It is surely
no accident that when he came to write his theory of politics
he relied heavily upon the virtues and abilities of this class.

What little information is available to us indicates that
Harrington was an exceptionally intelligent child, notable for
"his inclination and capacity to learn whatever was proposed
to him" and for "a kind of natural gravity" hardly to be expected in one so young. Having spent his early years at his
father's home in Lincolnshire, at the age of eighteen he became a Gentleman Commoner in Trinity College, Oxford.
There he studied chiefly under the famous apostate Catholic
theologian, William Chillingworth, whose most notable book,
The Religion of Protestants a Safe Way to Salvation (1637),
contained a lively defense of religious toleration, the influence
of which may be seen in Harrington's utterances on the same
subject. In addition to his general studies, Harrington devoted
himself particularly to learning foreign languages, apparently
with considerable success, since his writings exhibit a thor-
ough command of Greek, Latin, and Italian, as well as a working knowledge of Hebrew, French, and German. In April of
1630, Harrington's father died and shortly thereafter the
young man, who was now financially independent, determined to set out on a tour of the Continent—a form of education which even in the seventeenth century was conceived to
be peculiarly appropriate to the sons of aristocratic families.

Although he was only nineteen at the time of his departure,
Harrington's activities on the Continent suggest that he was

already deeply interested in politics. He traveled first to The Hague, where he became a close friend of Frederick V, the exiled Elector Palatine and "Winter King" of Bohemia, and of the elector's wife, Elizabeth, the daughter of James I. "This excellent Princess entertained him with extraordinary favor and civility on account of his Uncle the Lord Harrington, who had been her Governor; but particularly for the sake of his own Merit." [3] Charmed by the elector's family and moved by their unhappy plight, Harrington soon enlisted in the volunteer English regiment, led by the Earl of Craven, which was dedicated to the recovery of the Palatinate. The regiment marched from The Hague early in the year 1632 and reached Frankfurt-am-Main on February 10. There a parley between Frederick and Gustavus Adolphus revealed the Swedish king's unwillingness to co-operate with the elector and doomed the entire attempt to failure. Despite this rebuff at the hands of his putative ally, Frederick never lost hope that some day, with English aid, he might regain his throne, and to this end he commissioned the young Harrington to serve as his agent in England. Although Harrington did not return to England until considerably after the elector's death in 1632, in 1645 he did present to Parliament a petition which resulted in a grant of two thousand pounds on account "for the Supply of the urgent Necessities of the Prince Elector"—presumably Frederick's successor, the regent Louis Philip. As a result of this connection with the elector and his family, Harrington was personally involved in one of the most dramatic and poignant episodes of the Thirty Years' War; characteristically, both personal feelings and religious convictions dictated his support of the tragic champion of European Protestantism.

Harrington's sojourn at The Hague came during what has quite properly been called the "golden age" of the Netherlands. The unparalleled flowering of Dutch art and literature

[3] John Toland in "The Life of James Harrington," *The Oceana and Other Works of James Harrington, Esq.*, ed. by Toland et al. (London, 1747), p. xiv.

during this period, and the tremendous expansion of Dutch commerce in both the old world and the new, can hardly have failed to impress the young visitor—as indeed they impressed all his contemporaries. Nor can we suppose that he was unaware of the continuing struggle of the Protestant provinces which sought their independence of both foreign control and the attempted centralization of the House of Orange. When, after traveling through Flanders, Harrington reached France, the contrast must indeed have been striking. Just two years earlier, on November 11, 1630—the famous "Day of the Dupes"—Cardinal Richelieu had finally won his battle with Marie de' Medici for the support of the young Louis XIII, and by the time of Harrington's visit the cardinal was well on his way toward the creation of the rigidly centralized "great monarchy" that was to evoke the admiration of all Europe. Harrington, however, was unimpressed. Richelieu, he felt, had no understanding of the true principles of politics and consequently his "fame . . . hath been like the thunder, whereof we hear the noise, but can make no demonstration of the reason."

Finding little in France to detain him, Harrington traveled next to Italy, stopping first in the Rome of Urban VIII and then in Venice. Of all the places he was to visit, Venice had undoubtedly the greatest influence on the young Englishman's thought. Despite the fact that the greatness of the republic had declined considerably by the middle of the seventeenth century, Harrington was literally overwhelmed by what he saw there. John Toland, his earliest biographer, tells us that:

He preferred Venice to all other places in Italy, as he did its Government to all those in the whole world, it being in his opinion immutable by any external or internal causes. . . . Here he furnished himself with a collection of all the valuable Books in the Italian language, especially treating of politics, and contracted acquaintance with every one of whom he might receive and benefit by instruction or otherwise.[4]

[4] *Ibid.*, p. xv.

Typically, Harrington's chief concern was with the government of Venice; whatever the original purpose of his continental tour, its effect had clearly been to stimulate his interest in the world of politics. Thus Toland reports that "he was often heard to say that, before he left England he knew no more of Monarchy, Anarchy, Aristocracy, Democracy, Oligarchy or the like, than as hard words whereof he learned the signification in his Dictionary."

By the time of his return to England about 1635, Harrington's sympathies in his country's mounting constitutional crisis were firmly republican and antimonarchical. In view of this fact it is particularly interesting to note that he soon became an intimate friend of Charles I and accompanied the king to Scotland as a member of the Privy Chamber Extraordinary during the first Bishops' War (1639). John Aubrey, a contemporary, informs us that "the king loved his company, only he would not endure to hear of a Commonwealth; and Mr. Harrington passionately loved his Majesty." Perhaps because of the problems raised by this conflict of loyalties—personal devotion to the king versus intellectual commitment to republicanism—Harrington devoted himself during these troubled years chiefly to the affairs of his family, of which he was now the head, and to furthering his own education. "No man," he wrote in his first book, "can be a Politician, except he be first an Historian or a Traveller." Having already traveled extensively, he now set out to make himself an historian, assimilating in the process a vast body of political writings, ancient, medieval, and modern.

Almost nothing is known of Harrington's activities during the period of the first Civil War; the stories of his attempts to win a seat in Parliament have—like so much other alleged biographical information—proved unfounded. In January of 1647, when the Scottish army surrendered the captive Charles I to Parliament, a parliamentary commission was sent to bring the king from Newcastle to Holmby House, in Northampton, and perhaps to reach some sort of political agreement with him. As a supporter of the parliamentary cause, and at the same time a personal friend of the defeated king, Harrington joined the commission on its journey to Newcastle. Because of his previous acquaintance with Charles, he was chosen by the commissioners to wait on His Majesty; when the party reached Holmby House, he was made a Groom of the Bed-chamber and "had the good luck to grow very acceptable to the King, who much conversed with him about Books and Foreign Countries."

Harrington's behavior during the years from 1647 to 1649, years that were marked by growing extremism and intransi-geance on the part of both the royalists and their enemies, reveals his fundamental moderation and his constant desire to find some means of reconciling the king and the parlia-ment. Toland observes that "he served his Master [i.e., Charles I] with untainted fidelity, without doing any thing incon-sistent with the Liberty of his Country; and . . . he made use of his Interest with his Friends in Parliament to have matters accommodated for the satisfaction of all Parties." Un-fortunately, as Harrington was soon to learn, the time for compromise had passed. As a result of his supporting some of Charles' arguments during the negotiation of the abortive Treaty of Newport in 1648, Harrington was forcibly removed from the king's household, and was subsequently imprisoned for refusing to swear that he would not help Charles to escape from captivity. Ironically, it was Henry Ireton who finally arranged his release. On January 30, 1649, Harrington was present at Whitehall to witness the beheading of his "beloved friend," Charles I.

If Harrington had been nothing more than a doctrinaire republican theorist, the execution of Charles would have served to simplify his position considerably by removing one of the sources of his hopelessly divided loyalty. In fact, its effect was precisely the opposite. Depressed by the loss of his friend, and profoundly discouraged by the fanaticism that had caused this loss, Harrington "was observ'd to keep much in his Library, and more retired than usually, which was by his

friends a long time attributed to Melancholy or Discontent." [5]
At first, he determined to turn his back on the world of politics of which he had such unhappy experience, and toyed
briefly with the idea of becoming a poet, going so far as to
publish two translations from Virgil's *Aeneid* and *Eclogues*
in presentable (though undistinguished) English verse. It is
interesting that even here Harrington was unable entirely to
bridle his political imagination and intruded his beloved
theory of the balance of property in an extraneous ode, in a
footnote, and in various distortions of the texts he translated.
Before long, having discovered (or, rather, having been told)
that "his Muse was rough," Harrington abandoned any idea
of a purely literary career and, although he remained in retirement, turned to politics once again with the writing of his
magnum opus, *The Commonwealth of Oceana*. Later in his
life he explained the circumstances that led him to undertake
this project:

. . . I wrote under a Usurper, Oliver [Cromwell]. He having
started up into the Throne, his Officers (as pretending to be
for a Commonwealth) kept a murmuring, at which he told
them that he knew not what they meant, nor [did they] themselves; but let any one of them show him what they meant by
a Commonwealth (or that there was any such thing) and they
should see that he sought not himself: the Lord knew he
sought not himself, but to make good the Cause. Upon this
some sober men came to me and told me, if any man in England could show what a Commonwealth was, it was my self.
Upon this persuasion I wrote. . . .[6]

The writing of the *Oceana* required something more than
three years, beginning shortly after the establishment of the
Protectorate in 1653 and ending with the publication of the
book in the fall of 1656. As we have already seen, many of the
ideas presented in the *Oceana*—including its praise of the
Venetian constitution, its doctrine of the balance of property,
and its general republican bias—had been developed by

[5] *Ibid.*, p. xvii.
[6] *Ibid.*, p. xxxiv.

Harrington considerably earlier than this, but now for the first time he combined them in a coherent theoretical system and put forward this system as an answer to England's political problems.

III

The Commonwealth of Oceana is a long, tedious book, overburdened with trivial details and endless citations of historical and literary authorities. It is divided into four parts: (1) The Preliminaries; (2) The Council of Legislators; (3) The Model of the Commonwealth of Oceana; and (4) The Corollary. While the first of these parts consists of a general exposition of Harrington's theory of politics, the last three are concerned with the creation, the structure, and the operation of the government which Harrington believed should be established in England. If one uses the adjective "utopian" to describe visionary and impractical schemes, Harrington's *Oceana* was most certainly not intended as a utopian book; beneath the most transparent of disguises, its subject matter is clearly the political state of seventeenth-century England, as Harrington indicated in his introductory quotation from Horace: *"mutato nomine, de te Fabula narratur."* Despite his later statements about "the usurper Oliver," Harrington dedicated the *Oceana* to Cromwell and obviously hoped that the Lord Protector would use it as a handbook to guide him in the business of establishing a new government that would succeed where the Stuart monarchy, the short-lived Commonwealth, and the Protectorate had all failed. From the very beginning his hopes were disappointed. Far from seizing upon the *Oceana* as a blueprint, Cromwell first obstructed its publication and then, after his sister had interceded on Harrington's behalf, relented somewhat reluctantly on the understanding that "it was only a kind of Political Romance" quite unrelated to real events. Although Harrington explicitly offered to the Lord Protector the glory of being a new Lycurgus, Cromwell is said to have replied that "The Gentleman had like to trepan him out of his Power, but that what he got by the Sword he would not quit for a little paper Shot." This sounds very unlike Cromwell, and in all probability it was invented by Harrington or his friends, but in any case the Protector's decidedly cool reception of the book forced its author to revise his tactics; he could no longer rely, as Plato had done, on the appealingly simple device of a single omnipotent and all-wise Legislator.

The next four years Harrington devoted to the achievement of one purpose: the popularization of the ideas and proposals of his *Oceana*. With boundless energy and with considerable imagination, he repeated these ideas and proposals over and over again in books, in pamphlets, in dialogues, in comic essays, in illustrated broadsides, in petitions to Parliament, in collections of simple aphorisms, and, finally, in the meetings of his famous Rota Club. Although, as the years passed, he came increasingly to simplify his message and to strip away such superfluous details as descriptions of the uniforms to be worn by officials in the "equal commonwealth," Harrington made no fundamental change in his system after 1656. Like his equal commonwealth, this system had been created "at once and entire." The only important modifications that he would admit concerned the method of establishing the equal commonwealth, and these were clearly no more than minimal concessions to political reality. Harrington's tactics, and particularly the activities of the Rota Club—at which, Aubrey tells us, discussion was "the most ingeniose, and smart, that I ever heard, or expect to heare, and bandied with great eagerness; the arguments in the Parliament howse were but flatt to it. . . ." [7]—succeeded in winning for the theorist a considerable reputation among his contemporaries, but in their major purpose they failed utterly. Despite the presence in the last Protectorate Parliament of a large number of Harringtonians, and despite Harrington's truly feverish activity in the confused year following Oliver Cromwell's death, none of the proposals of the *Oceana* was adopted during the Interregnum. Finally, in 1660, the restoration of the Stuart mon-

[7] John Aubrey, *Brief Lives*, ed. Clark (Oxford, 1898), I, 289.

archy not only destroyed Harrington's last hope of immediate success, a hope founded upon the weakness of Richard Cromwell's government, but also effectively ended his career as a political figure. In the words of John Aubrey, "upon the unexpected turne upon Generall Monke's comeing-in [to re-establish the Long Parliament in February, 1660], all these aierie modells vanished." [8] Samuel Pepys attended the meeting of the Rota Club held on February 20, 1660, the very day on which the Long Parliament reassembled:

In the evening Simons and I to the Coffee Club, where nothing to do only I heard Mr. Harrington, and my Lord of Dorset and another Lord, talking of getting another place as the Cockpit, as they did believe it would come to something. After a small debate upon the question whether learned or unlearned subjects are the best the Club broke up very poorly, and I do not think they will meet any more. [9]

Pepys was right; this was, in fact, the last meeting of the Rota Club.

The remaining years of Harrington's life were marked by almost unrelieved tragedy, a gloomy record interesting chiefly as evidence of his persistent and almost uncanny ability to find disfavor with his country's rulers. Although Charles I had liked him personally, he would not hear of his political views. Oliver Cromwell had been profoundly suspicious of him, had tried to prevent the publication of the *Oceana,* and had steadfastly refused to play the glorious role Harrington had assigned him. Now Charles II, rightly recognizing Harrington's republican bias, wrongly accused him of plotting the overthrow of the restored monarchy and caused him to be thrown into the Tower of London in 1661. Although there is no evidence to indicate that Harrington was involved in any antimonarchical activities, his theory of politics led him freely to predict the imminent downfall of the Stuarts. Says Aubrey:

[8] *Ibid.,* I, 291.

[9] Samuel Pepys, *Diary,* ed. Wheatly (New York, n.d.), 1, 43.

I well remember, he severall times . . . sayd, "Well, the King will come in. Let him come-in, and call a Parliament of the greatest Cavaliers in England, so they be men of estates, and let them but sett seven years, and they will all turn Commonwealthe's men." [10]

Small wonder that Charles II, having summoned the so-called "Cavalier Parliament," felt that it would be wise to keep the author of such subversive statements in prison! Despite the lack of evidence against him, Harrington remained in prison for several years, an ordeal that destroyed both his health and reason. Finally, in 1677, he died and was buried in St. Margaret's Church, Westminster, next to the grave of Sir Walter Raleigh. It was typical of his life that an epitaph which had been written for him by his friend, Andrew Marvell, was thought to be politically offensive and was replaced by an innocuous Latin inscription. Actually, Harrington himself had provided a more fitting epitaph, when in 1659 he wrote in his *Art of Lawgiving:* "If this age fails me, the next will do me justice." His own age had most certainly failed him, but future ages were to atone for this, both by vindicating his political predictions and by adopting in large measure his political proposals.

IV

In so far as James Harrington is remembered at all today, he is remembered simply as a political theorist who emphasized the importance of economic conditions and who constructed an elaborate model of a state which he called *The Commonwealth of Oceana.* In a sense it is fitting that this should have been the judgment of posterity. Unquestionably Harrington believed that his most important discovery was the law of the "balance of property," and that his most significant practical contribution consisted in the description of that system of institutions known as the "equal commonwealth." In a broader sense, however, neither Harrington nor

10 Aubrey, *op. cit.,* I, 291.

the student of his writings can be wholly satisfied with this judgment. In addition to perpetuating the myth that Harrington was a man of one idea, it completely fails to recognize the two most interesting aspects of his political thought: his attempt to formulate a comprehensive and coherent science of politics, and his extraordinary success in understanding the fundamental political problems of his time. Thus, for example, Harrington's famous law of the "balance of property" was not simply the result of a happy guess or an isolated insight, but rather was one part of an extremely complex theoretical system designed to comprehend all of political reality. Similarly, the proposed institutions of the "equal commonwealth" were not dreamed up at random by Harrington's admittedly fertile imagination, but were designed with reference both to the laws of politics, as he understood them, and to the political condition of seventeenth-century Europe. The process of putting the parts of Harrington's theory back into their original places, of reintegrating his system, as it were, does not necessarily lead one to a more favorable estimate of his stature as a political theorist (although it may well serve this purpose), but it does result in a considerably more accurate and complete understanding of both the parts and the whole, and for this reason it is well worth undertaking.

In a passage that we have already noted, John Adams expressed his opinion that Harrington's doctrine of political balance "is as infallible a maxim in politics as that action and reaction are equal is in mechanics." This parallel between the Harringtonian principle and the Newtonian law of motion is in some respects an extremely suggestive and useful one, and it is most certainly one that would have pleased Harrington immensely. For although he lived a generation before the great physicist and was concerned with phenomena of a completely different order, Harrington was as much a child of the intellectual and scientific revolution of the seventeenth century as was Newton. Indeed, one may conveniently characterize Harrington's career by saying that throughout his life his primary concern was to apply to politics the tech-

niques that had proved so fruitful in the natural sciences,
creating (and also popularizing) a *science* of politics. Just as
the natural scientist postulated the existence of order in the
universe and sought to discover the principles that would
explain its operation, so Harrington argued that the task of
the student of politics was to reveal the underlying orderli-
ness of political life and to expound the laws that govern it.
In fact, Adams' parallel can be made even more exact by not-
ing that the very terminology which Harrington used was, to
a considerable extent, drawn from the natural sciences. The
notion of equilibrium, of balance, was taken directly from
physics; in order to demonstrate the relevance to politics of
this notion it was necessary, somehow, to reduce the elements
of political life to a form that would admit of quantitative
expression and of measurement on a common scale. Thus,
Harrington's preoccupation with the amount of property, the
number of voters, and the size of assemblies in various commonwealths may be taken as evidence of his determination to
"search for measurable elements among . . . phenomena, and
then search for relations between these measures of physical
quantities" [11]—a determination which Alfred North Whitehead has shown to be basic to the development of the natural
sciences in the seventeenth century.

If one attempts to carry the parallel between Newton's science and that of Harrington one step further, however, it
becomes quite misleading. Despite important similarities of
outlook, of terminology, and of method, it is perfectly clear
that Harrington did not propose to apply to politics the speculative, deductive method characteristic of the so-called "natural
philosophy." On the contrary, he repeatedly criticized Hobbes
(whom he considered in other respects "the best writer at this
day in the world" [12]) for attempting to erect an absolute monarchy "by geometry," and he never tired of expressing his
belief that the proper model for the new science of politics

[11] Alfred North Whitehead, *Science and the Modern World* (New York,
1948), p. 46.

[12] Harrington, *Prerogative of Popular Government*, in *Works*, p. 259.

was anatomy, the study of complex living organisms. Harring- ·
ton wrote, in his *Art of Lawgiving:* [13]

There is between the discourses of such as are commonly
called Natural Philosophers, and those of Anatomists, a large
difference; the former are facile, the latter difficult . . . but
the fearful and wonderful making, the admirable structure
and great variety of the parts of Man's Body, in which the
discourses of Anatomists are altogether conversant, are understood by so few, that I may say they are not understood by any.
Certain it is that the delivery of a Model of Government
(which either must be of no effect, or embrace all those
Muscles, Nerves, Arteries and Bones, which are necessary to
any function of a well-ordered Commonwealth) is no less than
political anatomy.

Inspired by the signal achievements of William Harvey (1578-
1657), the discoverer of the circulation of the blood, Harrington's "political anatomy" represented a deliberate attempt to
create a science of politics that would be able to deal effectively with an inherently complex subject matter, that would
be generally applicable without being so abstract as to have
no relation to the real world of politics. Harrington had little
sympathy for the amateurs of his day who were so carried
away by the wonders of natural science that they applied its
techniques indiscriminately to all fields; of the "virtuosi" who
were soon to found the Royal Society, he wryly observed, "they
had an excellent faculty of magnifying a Louse, and diminishing a Commonwealth." Magnifying a louse is a perfectly re-
spectable occupation for anyone who is so inclined, but the
very act of "diminishing" a commonwealth will inevitably obscure the wealth of detail which is essential to the operation
of any government, and will consequently prevent the discovery of meaningful and useful laws of political life. The reader
who is put off by the mass of trivia contained in Harrington's
discussion of various polities will do well to remember that
this passion for detail represents a deliberate attempt on the
author's part to avoid oversimplification and excessive abstrac-
tion.

[13] Harrington, *The Art of Lawgiving,* in *Works,* p. 429.

The application to politics of the techniques of natural science involved, among other things, a conscious decision to break away from the established patterns of political theory. In describing the principles which had guided his investigation of the circulatory system, William Harvey spoke of his determination "both to learn and to teach anatomy, not from books but from dissections; not from the positions of philosophers, but from the fabric of nature." When applied to his own field, this principle committed Harrington to the undertaking of an extensive empirical study of past and present governments, rejecting the technique of demonstration-by-authority that had characterized both the sciences and philosophical speculation during the preceding centuries, and attempting to arrive at valid generalizations by a process of induction. It is hardly necessary to say that Harrington believed this to be the only sure method of arriving at an understanding of political life. But any discussion of his methodology must also take into account the intensely practical nature of Harrington's interest in politics. Far from being a detached seeker after truth for its own sake, he devoted his life to the advocacy of certain political institutions and devices which he believed necessary to the well-being, indeed, to the survival, of his countrymen. Thus from the outset he was faced with a twofold task: first, he had to understand political reality and to discover remedies for the political ills of his day; having done this to his own satisfaction, he then had to convince his contemporaries of the accuracy of his analysis and the efficacy of his proposals. The second of these tasks was particularly troublesome in view of the fact that, in the seventeenth century, there no longer existed a commonly accepted body of doctrine or a universally respected canon of authorities to which one might appeal for support of his arguments. In a word, Harrington was confronted with the problem of how to prove anything to a generation fundamentally divided on the question of what constitutes "proof."

It is quite apparent that for Harrington himself "proof" was inseparably associated with the developing natural sciences. But what of those who found the techniques of science completely unimpressive and its conclusions quite unconvincing? Or, even more serious, what of those who considered that any attempt at demonstration without reference to divine revelation and received opinion was impertinent, if not actually blasphemous? What could Harrington say to convince such men: to convince the Puritan who demanded Scriptural precedent, the scholar who insisted that true wisdom resides only in the writings of classical antiquity, the churchman who called for citations from Aristotle and Aquinas? The problem was not, of course, unique with Harrington; it is a problem that must inevitably arise during an age of intellectual ferment, an age when (in Donne's phrase) "the new philosophy puts all in doubt." Nevertheless, it was a problem that Harrington could not afford to ignore if he wished to win wide support for his ideas. In order to solve it, he undertook to show that the principles of his new science of politics did not differ in substance either from divine purpose, as revealed in Scripture, or from the teachings of the classics.

The endeavor to reconcile "political anatomy" and the Bible took the relatively simple form of an assertion that "neither God, nor Christ, nor the Apostles, ever instituted any government ecclesiastical or civil upon any other principles than those only of Human Prudence." Thus the evidence available in the Bible—and particularly in the Old Testament—was not qualitatively different from that contained in other historical sources. Consequently, this biblical evidence comprised an important source of information to be used in the formulation of a science of politics, and no generalization could be considered satisfactory if it did not account for the political experience of the ancient Jews, as well as for that of all other peoples. Although Harrington had no sympathy for the Puritans whose political program began and ended with a demand that the institutions of the Old Testament be reproduced in all their details ("who imagines that a ship ought not to be built according to the art of the shipwright, or governed according to the compass, unless these be proved out of

Scripture"?),[14] he nevertheless was willing to admit the historical relevance of these institutions. But if the "commonwealth of Israel" was simply one in the long historical series of polities, in the sense that it conformed to the general laws of political life (i.e., to "Human Prudence"), it also clearly enjoyed a special status by virtue of its divine origin. For Harrington to have argued that the government of Israel was in any sense a "bad" government would almost literally have been suicidal; to have done this would not only have exposed him to charges of atheism, it would also have effectively undermined all confidence in his proposed political norms. Any system, be it ever so scientific, that resulted in an adverse judgment of God's handiwork was by that very fact damned in the eyes of most of Harrington's contemporaries. Quite understandably, then, Harrington claimed that the principles of good government which had been "first discovered to mankind by God himself in the fabric of the Commonwealth of Israel" were in fact rediscovered and vindicated by his own empirical investigations. But—and this is the central point—he insisted that these scientifically derived principles did not in any way depend on Scriptural authority for their validity. The precedent of the commonwealth of Israel was a sign of the correctness of his proposals, but in no sense was it for Harrington the decisive sign. Reversing what would surely have been the conventional order of argument in the seventeenth century, Harrington observed in his *Art of Lawgiving* [15] that "the principles of Human Prudence being good without proof of Scripture, are nevertheless such as are provable out of Scripture."

On the whole, it seems accurate to conclude that Harrington's undeniable preoccupation with religion and the Bible was dictated by considerations of expedience rather than by conviction. In the England of Laud and Cromwell, it was simply impossible to discuss politics without becoming embroiled in religious controversy (even the archmaterialist Hobbes felt

14 *Ibid.*, p. 395.
15 *Loc. cit.*

called upon to devote half of his *Leviathan* to religious questions), and Harrington, despite his fairly clear personal indifference, was determined that his theory of politics should emerge with the support of Scriptural authority. In a sense, the situation was the same with regard to classical sources. Here was another body of writings capable of eliciting great enthusiasm in an age still dominated by the spirit of the Renaissance; in particular, the connection between republican doctrine and the political practice of ancient Greece and Rome was inescapable.[16] The crucial difference lies in the fact that Harrington himself was among the most ardent admirers of the virtue, the uncorrupted purity of classical political institutions. Thus, while Bossuet's idea of *la politique tirée des propres paroles de l'Écriture sainte* would have seemed to him both overstated and impractical, the not-dissimilar idea of politics drawn from the very institutions of Periclean Athens and republican Rome appealed to him greatly. But even here Harrington was aware of the difficulties involved in taking the position that the problems of the corrupt modern world could be solved by the simple expedient of reproducing these ancient institutions. In the first place, it was quite clear that the governments of Greece and Rome had not been perfect; if they had been, they would never have been destroyed, and thus there would be no need to recreate them. Along the same lines, there was every reason to believe that if they were to be recreated in their original form they would simply suffer the same fate once again. Furthermore, even if one were to assume, as Harrington seems occasionally to have done, that the destruction of these noble polities was due solely to "external causes" rather than to some flaw in their constitutions, it would still be necessary to recognize, perhaps with sorrow, that seventeenth-century England simply was not sufficiently similar to Periclean Athens or republican Rome to make possible such a recreation. What, then, should be the policy of

[16] For an excellent treatment of this subject see Zera Fink, *The Classical Republicans* (Evanston, Ill., 1945).

one who profoundly admired and envied the political success of the ancients?

Harrington's answer was straightforward: such a person should make it his business to discover the fundamental *causes* of this success. Were the citizens of Athens public-spirited because of the bracing climate of Greece, or because they raised olives? Was the Roman republic virtuous because of its geographical location, or because its citizens wore togas? According to Harrington, these "explanations" cannot be dismissed simply because they seem far-fetched or illogical; because, in other words, we cannot immediately perceive any connection between government and climate, or costume, or diet. They can only be proven or disproven by an empirical, comparative study of political history and contemporary politics. Such a study, if it is managed properly, should enable us to isolate the essential determinants of political life, the fundamental causes of political success and failure, and to discard what Harrington once referred to as "accidents of no precedent to us." While he shared his contemporaries' view of history as, in essence, a decline from the golden age of classical antiquity through the ignorance and obscurantism of the "Gothic" Middle Ages to the anarchy and confusion of the modern age, and shared also their belief that the best hope of the modern world lay in a revival of "ancient prudence," Harrington used these familiar Renaissance arguments to justify something quite new: the creation of a science of politics modeled after the natural sciences. Mere antiquarianism, or a desire slavishly and uncritically to *imitate* the ancients, can lead to no good. This does not mean that one should ignore the examples of Greece and Rome, the "mines of ancient prudence"; on the contrary, one should study them with great care, remembering all the while, however, that "there is a difference between having the sense of a thing and making a right use of that sense." The latter—making a right use of our knowledge—necessarily involves the application of reason to historical data, the establishment of recurrent pat-

terns, and, finally, the discovery of causal relations. Thus, in
Harrington's system, the techniques of political anatomy were
in no way inconsistent with a profound regard for the institutions of the Greek *polis* and the Roman republic. On the
contrary, it was precisely those techniques which made possible the understanding, and thus the rational emulation, of
these institutions.

Our discussion of Harrington's treatment of religious and
classical sources reveals a fundamental ambivalence in his
thought, characteristic of the age in which he lived. Quite
simply, he was unable to decide whether the attractions of
innovation and novelty were preferable to the support of tradition and established authority; whether it was better to be
the founder of a new science or the "retriever" of ancient wisdom. On the one hand, he used the word "modern" (which
was just becoming current in English) in a uniformly derog-
atory sense; to call an idea or an institution "modern" was
automatically to condemn it in Harrington's eyes. On the
other hand, he insisted that the principles of politics, although they were "as ancient in Nature as her self," [17] were
nevertheless "as new in Art as my Writing." [18] The fact is
that Harrington, like many of his contemporaries, was excited
by the intellectual advances made in his lifetime, and particularly by the developing natural sciences which, in Francis
Bacon's words, promised to "extend more widely the limits of
the power and greatness of man," [19] but at the same time he
lacked the self-confidence that would have permitted him to
turn his back on divine revelation and the accumulated wisdom of the ages. One feels that he would have liked to strike
out boldly on his own, as William Harvey had done, relying
solely on the power of human reason and observation, but
that a combination of prudence and humility prevented his
doing so. Consequently, in the last analysis, one finds him

[17] Harrington, *Prerogative* . . . , in *Works*, p. 249.
[18] *Loc. cit.*
[19] Quoted in Basil Willey, *The 17th Century Background* (London,
1949), p. 40.

taking an essentially pragmatic position: any argument, any variety of evidence that serves to convince people, is useful, and should be employed. Thus, when Matthew Wren accused Harrington of falsely attributing his own theory of political balance to Aristotle, Harrington replied: "I who must either have the more of Authority, or the less of Competition in the point, shall lose neither way." [20] Although he was personally committed to the method which he described as political anatomy, Harrington's chief concern was to communicate to his contemporaries and to posterity certain substantive insights into the nature of political reality. He was so convinced of the urgency of this educational task that he was willing, finally, to subordinate to it all claims of originality.

In order to understand this sense of urgency, it is necessary to turn from Harrington's method to a brief consideration of the content of his theory of politics, and particularly his treatment of the crucial and closely related problems of sovereignty and constitutionalism. By far the most impressive aspect of Harrington's performance as a political theorist was his extraordinary success in viewing the constitutional crisis of mid-seventeenth-century England in its appropriate historical context and, consequently, in recognizing its fundamental nature and its general significance. Almost without exception, his contemporaries saw the English civil wars as essentially a conflict between the forces of "good" and the forces of "evil," assigning virtue and vice to the contestants in accordance with their own political and religious predilections. Unmoved by these partisan polemics, and despite his own clear commitment to the parliamentary cause, Harrington insisted that England's tragic experience was simply one manifestation of a great historical process, a process that transcended national boundaries. Quite simply, this was the collapse of the medieval political order and the emergence of the modern state—the pre-eminent political fact of the seventeenth century. Throughout Europe, the traditional system of government by king and estates had broken down in the face of religious conflict, and

[20] Harrington, *Prerogative* . . . , in *Works,* p. 292.

a decisive struggle had everywhere ensued, a struggle in which the issues were the existence and the location of ultimate political authority, of "sovereignty." This essential pattern Harrington perceived with startling clarity:

Your Gothic politicians [he wrote in his *Oceana*] seem unto me rather to have invented some new Ammunition, or Gunpowder, in their King and Parliament . . . than Government. For what is become of the Princes (a kind of people) in Germany? blown up. Where are the Estates, or the Power of the People in France? blown up. Where is that of the People in Aragon, and the rest of the Spanish kingdoms? blown up. On the other hand, where is the King of Spain's power in Holland? blown up. Where is that of the Austrian Princes in Switzerland? blown up. . . . Nor shall any man show a reason that will be holding in prudence why the people of [England] have blown up their King, but that their kings did not first blow up them. The rest is discourse for ladies.[21]

Although superficially they seemed quite different, Harrington recognized that the great political upheavals of his day—the Thirty Years' War in Germany, the wars of the Fronde in France, the English civil wars—were fundamentally similar in that each was a struggle between king and estates for political supremacy.

The discovery of this underlying pattern, although clearly a substantial step toward an understanding of seventeenth-century politics, was in fact only the beginning of Harrington's task. In the first place, it remained for him to isolate the factors which had caused this almost universal collapse of the old political order. This he did through his theory of the economic foundation of political power, a theory which holds that in the long run government must inevitably reflect the distribution of property in a community. Taking the English experience as typical, he attempted to show in some detail that the traditional system of "mixed monarchy" (i.e., government by "the king in parliament"), in which political power had been shared by the king, the nobility, and the clergy, had been founded upon a feudal distribution of property; this dis-

21 *Oceana* (1656 ed.), 152f.; see p. 143.

tribution had been so altered by the Tudors, Harrington argued, and property had come to be so widely dispersed, that some form of popular government must inevitably result. Although the details varied from country to country, the essential fact was that, by the seventeenth century, the economic conditions that had once made mixed monarchy feasible (indeed, natural) had everywhere ceased to exist. Consequently, it was inevitable that there should be a political realignment, that the possessors of property (whether monarchs, nobles, or "people") should once again achieve political supremacy. Thus, nothing short of the establishment of an appropriate "sovereign power"—a supreme political authority founded upon a solid economic base—could put an end to the horrors of internal anarchy that had characterized European politics during the first half of the seventeenth century.

Although his reasoning is clearly quite different from that of men like Bodin, Hobbes, and Spinoza, up to this point Harrington's conclusions seem very much like theirs: the avoidance of domestic strife requires a strong government, an absolute sovereign. The central point, however, is that Harrington carried the argument one step further. Having turned his back on the medieval tradition of divided authority, having, in effect, accepted the existence and the validity of the modern state, he went on to insist that this state must be constitutionalized, that its authority must somehow be subjected to law. In short, he believed that while the achievement of stability and order depended upon the existence of an absolute, sovereign power, it was the task of the political theorist to devise means which would prevent the arbitrary or selfish use of this power. Here, in this proposition, lies Harrington's most important contribution to political thought. It was expressed most clearly in his *Art of Lawgiving:* [22]

Where the Sovereign Power is not as entire and absolute as in Monarchy it self, there can be no government at all. It is not the limitation of Sovereign Power that is the cause of a Commonwealth, but such a libration [i.e., balance] or poise

[22] Harrington, *The Art of Lawgiving,* in *Works,* pp. 430-431.

of Orders, that there can be in the same no number of men having the interest, that can have the power; nor any number of men having the power, that can have the interest, to invade or disturb the government. As the Orders of Commonwealths are more approaching to, or remote from this Maxim . . . so are they more quiet or turbulent.

In this notion of a proper "libration" in the "Orders" of a commonwealth, we find the reason for Harrington's preoccupation with the most detailed aspects of institutional politics. Taking as his ideal "a government of laws and not of men," he believed that this ideal could be realized only through a skillful and delicate balancing and checking of power by a written constitution. Indirect elections, bicameralism, rotation in office, guarantees of religious liberty and liberty of conscience, the "agrarian law," the secret ballot, universal military training, free public education—all of these devices and many others, contained in the proposed constitution of the equal commonwealth of Oceana, were designed with one purpose in mind: to guarantee the proper use of the enormous power which had necessarily been concentrated in the hands of "that great Leviathan," the modern state. Harrington's own experience, as well as his study of history, had demonstrated to him that a popular government was no less likely to abuse this power than was the government of an autocrat. Consequently, he was convinced that the saying, "give us good men and they will make us good laws," was "the Maxim of a demagogue" and "exceeding fallible"; "give us good Orders and they will make us good men," on the other hand, was "the maxim of a Legislator and the most infallible in the politics." Small wonder, then, that throughout his career Harrington believed that

in the Art of Man (being the imitation of nature, which is the Art of God) there is nothing so like the first call of beautiful order out of chaos and confusion as the Architecture of a well-ordered Commonwealth.[23]

23 *Oceana* (1656 ed.), p. 287 (wrongly numbered 189; p. 207 in Liljegren's edition). The passage is a reference to the first sentence of Hobbes' Introduction to his *Leviathan*.

An exalted view of the political theorist's calling, perhaps, but one that led Harrington to create what David Hume called "the only valuable model of a commonwealth that has yet been offered to the public." [24]

Much as one would like to do so, it is unfortunately impossible to conclude with a brief, pithy statement of Harrington's "message" for posterity. This is true because of the fact that the essence of his theory consists largely in its very complexity and interrelatedness. Although Harrington was an amateur in the world of politics, no one can accuse him of having been a dilettante; despite his unfortunate modern reputation, he was most certainly not a man of one idea. On the contrary, his greatest desire was to construct a comprehensive science of politics, an intellectual system that would account for all political phenomena. In his continuing effort to achieve this goal, Harrington faced and sought to solve virtually all the problems that have occupied, and continue to occupy, the attention of political theorists. Since he was an exceptionally able observer, an avid and learned student of history, a competent though perhaps overly enthusiastic systematizer, and an extraordinarily honest man, his proposed solutions must be of considerable interest to anyone who shares his concern with the problems of politics. In particular, his efforts to develop a rational and historical justification for popular government, constitutional government, and individual liberty cannot be overlooked by those who, like Harrington, are committed to these values, or by those who wish to understand the intellectual foundations of the modern constitutional state.

CHARLES BLITZER

YALE UNIVERSITY
June, 1954

[24] Cf. David Hume's "Idea of a Perfect Commonwealth," reprinted from *Political Essays,* p. 146, "The Library of Liberal Arts #34" (The Liberal Arts Press, New York, 1953).

SELECTED BIBLIOGRAPHY

Note.—In addition to the works listed below, the reader is advised to consult the standard histories of political theory —such as Dunning's and Sabine's—and various books and articles dealing with aspects of seventeenth-century British history.

I HARRINGTON'S WORKS

The Commonwealth of Oceana. London, 1656. Also edited by Sven B. Liljegren (Heidelberg, 1924).

Pian Piano. . . . London, 1657.

An Essay upon Two of Virgil's Eclogues, tr. London, 1658.

The Prerogative of Popular Government. London, 1658.

The stumbling-block of Disobedience. . . . London, 1658.

Aphorisms Political. London, 1659.

The Art of Lawgiving. . . . London, 1659.

A Discourse shewing. . . . London, 1659.

A Discourse upon this saying. . . . London, 1659.

A Letter unto Mr. Stubs. London, 1659.

A Parallel. London, 1659.

Politicaster. London, 1659.

Pour enclouer le canon. London, 1659.

Seven Models of a Commonwealth or Brief Directions. . . . London, 1659.

Valerius and Publicola. London, 1659.

Virgil's Aeneid, Books iii-iv (tr.). London, 1659.

Political Discourses. London, 1660.

The Rota. London, 1660.

The Wayes and Meanes. . . . London, 1660.

A Word Concerning a House of Peers. London, 1660.

The Use and Manner of the Ballot. [Broadside, no date or place.]

The Oceana and His Other Works, ed. John Toland et al. London, 1700. Also Dublin, 1737 and 1758; London, 1747 and 1771.

II Works Pertaining Specifically to Harrington

A Contemporary Works:

Baxter, Richard, *A Holy Commonwealth, or political aphorisms opening the true Principles of Government.* London, 1659.

[Anon.], *The Benefit of the Ballot.* London, 1679[?].

[Anon.], *The Censure of the Rota upon Mr Milton's book, entitled, The readie and easie way to establish a free Commonwealth.* London, 1660.

[Anon.], *Chaos, or, a discourse.* London, 1659.

"R. G.", *A Copy of a letter from an officer of the army in Ireland.* London, 1656.

[Anon.], *Decrees and orders of the committee of safety of the Commonwealth of Oceana.* [no place] 1659.

[Anon.], *Eight and thirty queries.* . . . London, 1659.

Milton, John, *The Readie and easie way to establish a free Common-wealth.* London, 1660.

Rogers, John, *A Christian concertation with . . . Mr Harrington.* . . . London, 1659.

———, *Mr Harrington's parallel unparallel'd.* . . . London, 1659.

[Sprigg, William ?], *A Modest Plea for an equal commonwealth.* London, 1659.

Stubbe, Henry, *The Commonwealth of Oceana put in the ballance.* . . . London, 1660.

Wren, Matthew, *Considerations on Mr Harrington's Commonwealth of Oceana: restrained to the first part of the Preliminaries.* London, 1657.

———, *Monarchy Asserted, or the State of Monarchicall and Popular Government, in Vindication of the Considerations upon Mr Harrington's Oceana.* Oxford, 1659.

B More Recent Works:

Dwight, Theodore, "James Harrington and his influence upon American political institutions and political thought." *Political Science Quarterly,* Vol. II (1887), 1ff.

Gough, J. W., "Harrington and contemporary thought." *P.S.Q.,* XLV (1930), 395-404.

Kroebner, Richard, "Die Geschichtslehre James Harringtons." *Geist und Gesellschaft,* III (Breslau, 1927-1928), 4-21.

————, "Oceana." *Englische studien,* Bd. 68 (Leipzig, 1934), 358-396.

Lesueur, Theodore, "A French draft constitution of 1792 modelled on James Harrington's *Oceana.*" Edited and with an introductory essay by S. B. Liljegren. Lund, 1932.

Levett, A. E., "James Harrington." *Social and Political Ideas of the sixteenth and seventeenth centuries,* ed., F. J. C. Hearnshaw. New York, 1949, pp. 174-203.

Liljegren, Sven Bodmer, "Harrington and Leibnitz." *Studies in English Philology* (Minneapolis, 1929), pp. 414-426.

————, "Some notes on the name of James Harrington's *Oceana.*" *Probleme der englischen Sprache und Kultur* (Heidelberg, 1925), pp. 231-249.

Smith, H. F. Russell, *Harrington and his Oceana; a study of a seventeenth century utopia and its influence in America.* Cambridge, 1914.

Tawney, R. H., "Harrington's interpretation of his age." *Proceedings of the British Academy,* XXVII (London, 1941).

Trevor, Daphne, "Some sources of the constitutional theory of the abbe Sieyes: Harrington & Spinoza." *Politica,* III (London, 1935), 325-342.

Wershofen, Christian, "James Harrington und sein Wunschbild vom germanischen Staate." *Bonner Studien zur Englischen Philologie,* XXVI (Bonn, 1935).

A SYSTEM OF POLITICS
DELINEATED IN SHORT
AND EASY APHORISMS

A SYSTEM OF POLITICS

Delineated in Short and Easy Aphorisms

The following is the complete text of Harrington's *System of Politics*. John Toland, the first editor of Harrington's works, tells this story of its composition: "About this time he was busy in reducing his Politics into short and easy Aphorisms, yet methodically digested in their natural order, and suited to the most vulgar capacities. . . . While he was putting the last hand to this System, and as an innocent man apprehensive of no danger, he was by an order from the King, on the 28th of December 1661, seized . . . and committed to the Tower of London for treasonable designs and practices. He had the written sheets of his Aphorisms then lying loose on the table before him, and understanding that they intended to carry them to the Council, he begged the favor that he might stitch them together; which was granted, and so removed with some other papers to Whitehall. I have that Manuscript now in my hands," Toland continues, "and another copy of the same which was given me by one of his acquaintance, from both of which I have printed it among the rest of his Works. It is a complete System of Politics, and discovers the true springs of the rise, temper and dissolution of all sorts of governments, in a very brief and perspicuous manner."

The *System of Politics* was first published in Toland's 1700 edition of Harrington's *Works*. It is in many ways its author's most impressive product; the ideas are better organized and the style more lucid than in any of Harrington's earlier writings. In addition, it is particularly interesting for its discussion of reason of state. (The text may be found on pages 496-514 of the 1747 *Collected Works*, 3rd edition.)

I. OF GOVERNMENT

1. A people is either under a state of civil government or in a state of civil war, or neither under a state of civil government nor in a state of civil war.

2. Civil government is an art whereby a people rule them-selves or are ruled by others.

3. The art of civil government in general is twofold: national or provincial.

4. National government is that by which a nation is governed independently, or within itself.

5. Provincial government is that by which a province is governed dependently, or by some foreign prince or state.

6. A people is neither governed by themselves nor by others, but by reason of some external principle thereto forcing them.

7. Force is of two kinds, natural and unnatural.

8. Natural force consists in the vigor of principles and their natural, necessary operations.

9. Unnatural force is an external or adventitious opposition to the vigor of principles and their necessary working which, from a violation of nature, is called violence.

10. National government is an effect of natural force, or vigor.

11. Provincial government is an effect of unnatural force, or violence.

12. The natural force which works or produces national government (of which only I shall speak hereafter) consists in riches.

13. The man that cannot live upon his own must be a serv-ant; but he that can live upon his own may be a freeman.

14. Where a people cannot live upon their own, the government is either monarchy or aristocracy; where a people can live upon their own, the government may be democracy.

15. A man that could live upon his own may yet, to spare his own and live upon another, be a servant; but a people that can live upon their own cannot spare their own and live upon another, but (except they be not servants; that is, except they come to a democracy) they must waste their own by maintaining their master's or by having others to live upon them.

16. Where a people that can live upon their own imagine that they can be governed by others and not lived upon by

such governors, it is not the genius of the people; it is the mistake of the people.

17. Where a people that can live upon their own will not be governed by others lest they should be lived upon by others, it is not the mistake of the people; it is the genius of the people.

18. Of government there are three principles: matter, privation, and form.

II. OF THE MATTER OF GOVERNMENT

1. That which is the matter of government is what we call an estate, be it in lands, goods, or money.

2. If the estate be more in money than in land, the port or garb [1] of the owner goes more upon his money than his lands, which with private men is ordinary but with nations (except such only as live more upon their trade than upon their territory) is not to be found. For which cause overbalance of riches in money or goods, as to the sequel [i.e., remainder] of these aphorisms, is altogether omitted.

3. If the estate be more in land than in goods or money, the garb and port of the owner (whether a man or a nation) goes more, if not altogether, upon his land.

4. If a man has some estate he may have some servants or a family, and consequently some government or something to govern; if he has no estate he can have no government.

5. Where the eldest of many brothers has all or so much that the rest for their livelihood stand in need of him, that brother is as it were prince in that family.

6. Where of many brothers the eldest has but an equal share, or not so inequal as to make the rest stand in need of him for their livelihood, that family is as it were a commonwealth.

---

[1] "Port," manner or style of living; "garb," fashion or style of dress, etc. esp. that distinctive of rank or standing. Harrington uses these words to signify status, both economic and social.

7. Distribution of shares in land as to the three grand interests, the king, the nobility, and the people, must be equal or inequal.

8. Equal distribution of land, as if one man or a few men have one half of the territory and the people have the other half, causes privation of government and a state of civil war, for the lord or lords on the one side being able to assert their pretension or right to rule, and the people on the other their pretension or right to liberty; that nation can never come under any form of government till that question be decided; and property being not by any law to be violated or moved, any such question cannot be decided but by the sword only.

9. Unequal distribution of shares in land as to the three grand interests, or the whole land in any one of these, is that which causes one of these three to be the predominant interest.

10. All government is interest, and the predominant interest gives the matter or foundation of the government.

11. If one man has the whole or two parts in three of the whole land or territory, the interest of one man is the predominant interest and causes absolute monarchy.

12. If a few men have the whole or two parts in three of the whole land or territory, the interest of the few or of the nobility is the predominant interest and, were there any such thing in nature, would cause a pure aristocracy.

13. It being so that pure aristocracy or the nobility, having the whole or two parts in three of the whole land or territory without a moderator or prince to balance them, is a state of war in which everyone as he grows eminent or potent aspires to monarchy; and that not any nobility can have peace or can reign without having such a moderator or prince as on the one side they may balance or hold in from being absolute, and on the other side may balance or hold them and their factions from flying out into arms, it follows that if a few men have the whole or two parts in three of the whole land or territory, the interest of the nobility being the predominant interest must of necessity produce regulated monarchy.

14. If the many or the people have the whole or two parts

in three of the whole land or territory, the interest of the many or of the people is the predominant interest and causes democracy.

15. A people neither under absolute or under regulated monarchy, nor yet under democracy, are under a privation of government.

III. OF THE PRIVATION OF GOVERNMENT

1. Where a people are not in a state of civil government but in a state of civil war, or where a people are neither under a state of civil government nor under a state of civil war, there the people are under privation of government.

2. Where one man, not having the whole or two parts in three of the whole land or territory, yet assumes to himself the whole power, there the people are under privation of government, and this privation is called "tyranny."

3. Where a few men, not having the whole or about two parts in three of the whole land or territory, yet assume to themselves the whole power, there the people are under privation of government, and this privation is called "oligarchy."

4. Where the many or the people, not having the whole or two parts in three of the whole land or territory, yet assume to themselves the whole power, there the people are under privation of government, and this privation is called "anarchy."

5. Where the tyranny, the oligarchy, or the anarchy, not having in the land or territory such a full share as may amount to the truth of government, have nevertheless such a share in it as may maintain an army, there the people are under privation of government, and this privation is a state of civil war.

6. Where the tyranny, the oligarchy, or the anarchy have not any such share in the land or territory as may maintain an army, there the people are in privation of government; which privation is neither a state of civil government nor a state of civil war.

7. Where the people are neither in a state of civil govern-

ment nor in a state of civil war, there the tyranny, the oligarchy, or the anarchy cannot stand by any force of nature because it is void of any natural foundation, nor by any force of arms because it is not able to maintain an army, and so it must fall away of itself through the want of a foundation or be blown up by some tumult. And in this kind of privation the matter or foundation of a good orderly government is ready and in being, and there wants nothing to the perfection of the same but proper superstructures or form.

IV. OF THE FORM OF GOVERNMENT

1. That which gives the being, the action, and the denomination to a creature or thing is the form of that creature or thing.

2. There is in form something that is not elementary but divine.

3. The contemplation of form is astonishing to man and has a kind of trouble or impulse accompanying it that exalts his soul to God.

4. As the form of a man is the image of God, so the form of a government is the image of man.

5. A man is both a sensual and a philosophical creature.

6. Sensuality in a man is when he is led only as are the beasts, that is, no otherwise than by appetite.

7. Philosophy is the knowledge of divine and human things.

8. To preserve and defend himself against violence is natural to man as he is a sensual creature.

9. To have an impulse or to be raised upon contemplation of natural things to the adoration or worship of God is natural to man as he is a philosophical creature.

10. Formation of government is the creation of a political creature after the image of a philosophical creature, or it is an infusion of the soul or faculties of a man into the body of a multitude.

11. The more the soul or faculties of a man (in the manner

of their being infused into the body of a multitude) are refined or made incapable of passion, the more perfect is the form of government.

12. Not the refined spirit of a man, or of some men, is a good form of government; but a good form of government is the refined spirit of a nation.

13. The spirit of a nation (whether refined or not refined) can never be wholly saint nor atheist: not saint because the far greater part of the people is never able in matters of religion to be their own leaders, nor atheists because religion is every whit as indelible a character in man's nature as reason.

14. Language is not a more natural intercourse between the soul of one man and another than religion is between God and the soul of a man.

15. As not this language nor that language, but some language, so not this religion nor that religion, yet some religion is natural to every nation.

16. The soul of government as the true and perfect image of the soul of man is every whit as necessarily religious as rational.

17. The body of a government as consisting of the sensual part of man is every whit as preservative and defensive of itself as sensual creatures are of themselves.

18. The body of a man, not actuated or led by the soul, is a dead thing out of pain and misery; but the body of a people, not actuated or led by the soul of government, is a living thing in pain and misery.

19. The body of a people, not led by the reason of the government, is not a people but a herd; not led by the religion of the government is at an inquiet and an uncomfortable loss in itself; not disciplined by the conduct of the government is not an army for defense of itself but a rout; not directed by the laws of the government has not any rule of right; and without recourse to the justice or judicatories of the government has no remedy of wrongs.

20. In contemplation of and in conformity to the soul of man, as also for supply of those his necessities which are not

otherwise supplied or to be supplied by nature, form of government consists necessarily of these five parts: the civil, which is the reason of the people; the religious, which is the comfort of the people; the military, which is the captain of the people; the laws, which are the rights of the people; and the judicatories, which are the avengers of their wrongs.

21. The parts of form in government are as the offices in a house, and the orders of a form of government are as the orders of a house or family.

22. Good orders make evil men good and bad orders make good men evil.

23. Oligarchists (to the end they may keep all others out of the government), pretending themselves to be saints, do also pretend that they in whom lust reigns are not fit for reign or for government. But *libido dominandi*, the lust of government, is the greatest lust, which also reigns most in those that have least right, as in oligarchists; for many a king and many a people have and had unquestionable right, but an oligarchist never. Whence from their own argument, the lust of government reigning most in oligarchists, it undeniably follows that oligarchists of all men are least fit for government.

24. As in houses not differing in the kinds of their offices, the orders of families differ much, so the difference of form in different governments consists not in the kinds or number of the parts, which in every one is alike, but in the different ways of ordering those parts. And as the different orders of a house arise for the most part from the quantity and quality of the estate by which it is defrayed or maintained, according as it is in one or more of the family as proprietors, so it is also in a government.

25. The orders of the form, which are the manners of the mind of the government, follow the temperament of the body or the distribution of the lands or territories and the interests thence arising.

26. The interest of arbitrary monarchy is the absoluteness of the monarch; the interest of regulated monarchy is the greatness of the nobility; the interest of democracy is the

felicity of the people—for in democracy the government is for the use of the people, and in monarchy the people are for the use of the government, that is, of one lord or more.

27. The use of a horse without his provender or of the people without some regard had to the necessities of human nature can be none at all; nor are those necessities of nature in any form whatsoever to be otherwise provided for than by those five parts already mentioned, for which cause every government consists of five parts: the civil, the religious, the military, the laws, and the judicatories.

V. OF FORM IN THE CIVIL PART

1. Those naturalists that have best written of generation do observe that all things proceed from an egg and that there is in every egg a *punctum saliens,* or a part first moved, as the purple speck observed in those of hens, from the working whereof the other organs or fit members are delineated, distinguished, and wrought into one organical body.

2. A nation without government or fallen into privation of form is like an egg unhatched, and the *punctum saliens,* or first mover from the corruption of the former to the generation of the succeeding form, is either a sole legislator or a council.

3. A sole legislator, proceeding according to art or knowledge, produces government in the whole piece at once and in perfection. But a council (proceeding not according to art, or what in a new case is necessary or fit for them, but according to that which they call the "genius of the people" still hankering after the things they have been used to, or their old customs, how plain soever it be made in reason that they can no longer fit them) make patching work and are ages about that which is very seldom or never brought by them to any perfection, but commonly comes by the way to ruin, leaving the noblest attempts under reproach and the authors of them exposed to the greatest miseries while they live, if not their

memories when they are dead and gone to the greatest infamy.

4. If the *punctum saliens* or first mover in generation of the form be a sole legislator, his proceeding is not only according to nature, but according to art also, and begins with the delineation of distinct orders or members.

5. Delineation of distinct orders or members (as to the form of government) is a division of the territory into fit precincts once stated for all, and a formation of them to their proper offices and functions according to the nature or truth of the form to be introduced.

6. Precincts in absolute monarchy are commonly called "provinces," and as to the delineation or stating of them they may be equal or inequal. Precincts in regulated monarchy, where the lords or nobility as to their titles or estates ought not to be equal, but to differ as one star differs from another in glory, are commonly called "counties," and ought to be inequal. Precincts in democracy, where without equality in the electors there will hardly be any equality in the elected, or where without equality in the precincts it is almost if not altogether impossible there should be equality in the commonwealth, are properly called "tribes," and ought by all means to be equal.

7. Equality or parity has been represented an odious thing and made to imply the leveling of men's estates; but if a nobility, how inequal soever in their estates or titles (yet to come to the truth of aristocracy), must as to their votes or participation in the government be *pares regni*—that is to say, peers or in parity among themselves—as well likewise the people (to attain to the truth of democracy) may be peers or in parity among themselves, and yet not as to their estates be obliged to leveling.

8. Industry of all things is the most accumulative, and accumulation of all things hates leveling. The revenue, therefore, of the people being the revenue of industry, though some nobility (as that of Israel or that of Lacedaemon) may be found to have been levelers, yet not any people in the world.

9. Precincts being stated are in the next place to be formed

to their proper offices and functions according to the truth of the form to be introduced, which in general is to form them, as it were, into distinct governments and to endow them with distinct governors.

10. Governments or governors are either supreme or subordinate. For absolute monarchy to admit in its precincts any government or governors that are not subordinate but supreme were a plain contradiction. But that regulated monarchy and democracy may do it is seen in the princes of Germany and in the cantons of Switzerland. Nevertheless, these being governments that have derived this not from the wisdom of any legislator but from accident and an ill disposition of the matter whereby they are not only incapable of greatness but even of any perfect state of health, they come not under the consideration of art, from which they derive not, but of chance, to which we leave them. And, to speak according to art, we pronounce that as well in democracy and in regulated as in absolute monarchy governors and governments in the several divisions ought not to be sovereignties, but subordinate to one common sovereign.

11. Subordinate governors are at will, or for life, or upon rotation or changes.

12. In absolute monarchy the governors of provinces must either be at will or upon rotation, or else the monarch cannot be absolute. In regulated monarchy the governors of the counties may be for life or hereditary, as in counts or lords, or for some certain term and upon rotation, as in viscounts or sheriffs. In democracy [either] the people are servants to their governors for life and so cannot be free, or the governors of the tribes must be upon rotation and for some certain term, excluding the party [i.e., person] that have borne the magistracy for that term from being elected into the like again till an equal interval or vacation be expired.

13. The term in which a man may administer government to the good of it and not attempt upon it to the harm of it is the fittest term of bearing magistracy; and three years in a magistracy described by the law, under which a man has lived

and which he has known by the carriage or practice of it in others, is a term in which he cannot attempt upon his government for the hurt of it, but may administer it for the good of it, though such a magistracy should consist of divers functions.

14. Governors in subordinate precincts have commonly three functions: the one civil, the other judicial, and the third military.

15. In absolute monarchy the government consists of one beglerbeg, or governor for three years, with his council or divan for civil matters and his guard of janizaries and spahis, that is of horse and foot [soldiers], with power to levy and command the timariots or military farmers.[2]

16. In regulated monarchy the government of a county consists of one count or lord for life, or of one viscount or sheriff for some limited term, with power in certain civil and judicial matters, and to levy and command the *posse comitatus*.[3]

17. In democracy the government of a tribe consists of one council or court, in one-third part elected annually by the people of that tribe for the civil, for the judicial, and for the military government of the same, and also to preside at the election of deputies in that tribe toward the annual supply in one-third part of the common and sovereign assemblies of the whole commonwealth; that is to say, of the senate and of the popular assembly, in which two these tribes, thus delineated and distinguished into proper organs or fit members to be actuated by those sovereign assemblies, are wrought up again by connection into one entire and organical body.

18. A parliament of physicians would never have found out the circulation of the blood, nor could a parliament of poets have written Virgil's *Aeneid;* of this kind, therefore, in the

[2] The terms used here are all taken from the Turkish monarchy, which was always for Harrington the classic example of absolute monarchy.

[3] The use of these English terms indicates Harrington's view of the traditional government of England between 1066 and 1640 as typical of regulated, or limited, monarchy. *Posse comitatus,* literally "the power of the county," is the origin of the western American term "posse," which indicates precisely its meaning.

formation of government is the proceeding of a sole legislator. But if the people without a legislator set upon such work by a certain instinct that is in them, they never go further than to choose a council, not considering that the formation of government is as well a work of invention as of judgment, and that a council, though in matters laid before them they may excel in judgment, yet invention is as contrary to the nature of a council as it is to musicians in consort who can play and judge of any air that is laid before them, though to invent a part of music they can never well agree.

19. In councils there are three ways of result [i.e., decision] and every way of result makes a different form. A council with the result in the prince makes absolute monarchy. A council with the result in the nobility, or where without the nobility there can be no result, makes aristocracy or regulated monarchy. A council with the result in the people makes democracy. There is a fourth kind of result or council which amounts not to any form, but to privation of government, that is, a council not consisting of a nobility and yet with the result in itself, which is rank oligarchy; so the people, seldom or never going any further than to elect a council without any result but itself, instead of democracy introduce oligarchy.

20. The ultimate result in every form is the sovereign power. If the ultimate result be wholly and only in the monarch, that monarchy is absolute. If the ultimate result be not wholly and only in the monarch, that monarchy is regulated. If the result be wholly and only in the people, the people are in liberty or the form of government is democracy.

21. It may happen that a monarchy founded upon aristocracy, and so as to the foundation regulated, may yet come by certain expedients or intrusions (as at this day in France and in Spain) as to the administration of it to appear or be called absolute, of which I shall treat more at large when I come to speak of "Reason of State," or of administration.

22. The ultimate result in the whole body of the people, if the commonwealth be of any considerable extent, is altogether

impracticable; and if the ultimate result be but in a part of the people, the rest are not in liberty nor is the government democracy.

23. As a whole army cannot charge at one and the same time, yet is so ordered that everyone in his turn comes up to give the charge of the whole army, so, though the whole people cannot give the result at one and the same time, yet they may be so ordered that everyone in his turn may come up to give the result of the whole people.

24. A popular assembly, rightly ordered, brings up everyone in his turn to give the result of the whole people.

25. If the popular assembly consists of one thousand or more, annually changeable in one-third part by new elections made in the tribes by the people, it is rightly ordered; that is to say, so constituted that such an assembly can have no other interest whereupon to give the result than that only which is the interest of the whole people.

26. But in vain is the result where there is no matter to resolve upon; and where maturity of debate has not preceded, there is not yet matter to resolve upon.

27. Debate to be mature cannot be managed by a multitude, and result to be popular cannot be given by a few.

28. If a council capable of debate has also the result, it is oligarchy. If an assembly capable of the result has debate also, it is anarchy. Debate in a council not capable of result, and result in an assembly not capable of debate, is democracy.

29. It is not more natural to a people in their own affairs to be their own choosers than upon that occasion to be provided of their learned council; in so much that the saying of Pacuvius that "either a people is governed by a king or councilled by a senate" is universally approved.[4]

30. Where the senate has no distinct interest, there the people are councillable and venture not upon debate; where the senate has any distinct interest, there the people are not councillable but fall into debate among themselves and so into confusion.

4 Pacuvius (220-130 B.C.) was a Roman tragedian under the Republic.

31. Of senates there are three kinds: first, a senate eligible out of the nobility only, as that of Rome, which will not be contented to be merely the council of the people, but will be contending that they are lords of the people, never quitting their pretensions till they have ruined the commonwealth; secondly, a senate elected for life, as that of Sparta, which will be a species of nobility and will have a kind of Spartan king and a senate upon rotation, which being rightly constituted is quiet and never pretends more than to be the learned council of the people;

32. Thirdly, three hundred senators, for example, changeable in one-third part of them annually by new elections in the tribes and constituted a senate to debate upon all civil matters; to promulgate to the whole nation what they have debated, this promulgation to be made some such convenient time before the matters by them debated are to be proposed, that they may be commonly known and well understood, and then to propose the same to the result of the popular assembly, which only is to be the test of every public act, is a senate rightly ordered.

Form of government (as to the civil part) being thus completed is summed up in the three following Aphorisms:

33. Absolute monarchy (for the civil part of the form) consists of distinct provinces under distinct governors equally subordinate to a *grand signior* or sole lord, with his council or divan debating and proposing, and the result wholly and only in himself.

34. Regulated monarchy (for the civil part of the form) consists of distinct principalities or counties under distinct lords or governors, which, if rightly constituted, are equally subordinate to the king and his peerage, or to the king and his estates assembled in parliament, without whose consent the king can do nothing.

35. Democracy (for the civil part of the form), if rightly constituted, consists of distinct tribes under the government of distinct magistrates, courts, or councils, regularly changeable

in one-third part upon annual elections and subordinate to a senate consisting of not above three hundred senators and to a popular assembly consisting of not under a thousand deputies, each of these also regularly changeable in one-third part upon annual elections in the tribes, the senate having the debate and the popular assembly the result of the whole commonwealth.

VI. OF FORM IN THE RELIGIOUS PART

1. Form for the religious part either admits of liberty of conscience in the whole or in part, or does not admit of liberty of conscience at all.

2. Liberty of conscience entire or in the whole is where a man, according to the dictates of his own conscience, may have the free exercise of his religion without impediment to his preferment or employment in the state.

3. Liberty of conscience in part is where a man, according to the dictates of his conscience, may have the free exercise of his religion, but if it be not the national religion, he is thereby incapable of preferment or employment in the state.

4. Where the form admits not of the free exercise of any other religion except that only which is national, there is no liberty of conscience.

5. Men who have the means to assert liberty of conscience have the means to assert civil liberty, and will do it if they are oppressed in their consciences.

6. Men participating in property or in employment, civil or military, have the means to assert liberty of conscience.

7. Absolute monarchy, being sole proprietor, may admit of liberty of conscience to such as are not capable of civil or military employment, and yet not admit of the means to assert civil liberty, as the Greek Christians under the Turks, who, though they enjoy liberty of conscience, cannot assert civil liberty because they have neither property nor any civil or military employments.

8. Regulated monarchy, being not sole proprietor, may not

admit naturally of liberty of conscience lest it admits of the means to assert civil liberty, as was lately seen in England by pulling down the bishops who, for the most part, are one half of the foundation of regulated monarchy.

9. Democracy, being nothing but entire liberty, and liberty of conscience without civil liberty or civil liberty without liberty of conscience being but liberty by halves, must admit of liberty of conscience both as to the perfection of its present being and as to its future security: as to the perfection of its present being, for the reasons already shown, or that she do not enjoy liberty by halves; and for future security, because this excludes absolute monarchy, which cannot stand with liberty of conscience in the whole, and regulated monarchy, which cannot stand safely with it in any part.

10. If it be said that in France there is liberty of conscience in part, it is also plain that while the hierarchy is standing this liberty is falling, and that if it ever comes to pull down the hierarchy, it pulls down that monarchy also, wherefore the monarchy or hierarchy will be beforehand with it if they see their true interest.

11. The ultimate result in monarchy being that of one man or of a few men, the national religion in monarchy may happen not to be the religion of the major part of the people; but the result in democracy being in the major part of the people, it cannot happen but that the national religion must be that of the major part of the people.

12. The major part of the people, being in matters of religion unable to be their own leaders, will in such cases therefore have a public leading; or, being debarred of their will in that particular, are debarred of their liberty of conscience.

13. Where the major part of the people is debarred of their liberty by the minor, there is neither liberty of conscience nor democracy, but spiritual or civil oligarchy.

14. Where the major part is not debarred of their liberty of conscience by the minor, there is a national religion.

15. National religion is either coercive or not coercive.

16. Religion is not naturally subservient to any corrupt or

worldly interest, for which cause to bring it into subjection to interest it must be coercive.

17. Where religion is coercive or in subjection to interest, there is not or will not long continue to be the true religion.

18. Where religion is not coercive nor under subjection to any interest, there it either is or has no obstruction why it may not come to be the true religion.

19. Absolute monarchy pretends to infallibility in matters of religion, employs not any that is not of its own faith, and punishes its apostates by death without mercy.

20. Regulated monarchy comes not much short of the same pretense, but consisting of proprietors, and such as if they dissent have oftentimes the means to defend themselves, it does not therefore always attain to the exercise of the like power.

21. Democracy pretends not to infallibility, but is in matters of religion no more than a seeker, not taking away from its people their liberty of conscience but educating them, or so many of them as shall like of it, in such a manner or knowledge in divine things as may render them best able to make use of their liberty of conscience, which it performs by the national religion.

22. National religion, to be such, must have a national ministry or clergy.

23. The clergy is either a landed or a stipendiated clergy.

24. A landed clergy attaining to one-third of the territory is aristocracy and therefore equally incompatible with absolute monarchy and with democracy, but to regulated monarchy for the most part [it] is such a supporter as in that case it may be truly enough said that NO BISHOP, NO KING.[5]

25. The sovereignty of the prince in absolute monarchy and of the people in democracy admitting not of any counterpoise,

[5] Harrington here cites the singularly apt phrase coined by James I to express the mutual dependence of the Stuart monarchy and the Church of England. As Godfrey Davies has said, "The Stuart system of government would have collapsed ignominiously early in the century but for the support of the hierarchy, and Jacobean and Caroline bishops would, but for the royal favor, have been called to account before the Long Parliament met." Davies, *The Early Stuarts* (Oxford, 1938), p. 69.

in each of these the clergy ought not to be landed; the laborer nevertheless being worthy of his hire, they ought to be stipendiated.

26. A clergy well landed is to regulated monarchy a very great glory, and a clergy not well stipendiated is to absolute monarchy or to democracy as great an infamy.

27. A clergy, whether landed or stipendiated, is either hierarchical or popular.

28. A hierarchical clergy is a monarchical ordination; a popular clergy receives ordination from election by the people.

Form of government (as to the religious part) being thus completed is summed up in the three following Aphorisms:

29. Absolute monarchy (for the religious part of the form) consists of a hierarchical clergy and of an Al Koran (or some book received in the nature of scripture) interpretable by the prince only and his clergy, willingly permitting to them that are not capable of employments a liberty of conscience.

30. Regulated monarchy (for the religious part of the form) consists of an aristocratical hierarchy, of the liturgy, and of the Holy Scriptures (or some such book received for a rule of faith) interpretable only by the clergy, not admitting liberty of conscience except through mere necessity.

31. Democracy (for the religious part of the form) consists of a popular clergy, of the Scriptures (or some other book acknowledged divine), with a directory for the national religion and a council for the equal maintenance both of the national religion and of the liberty of conscience.

VII. OF FORM IN THE MILITARY PART

1. A man may perish by the sword, yet no man draws the sword to perish, but to live by it.

2. So many ways as there are of living by the sword, so many ways there are of a militia.

3. If a prince be lord of the whole or of two parts in three of the whole territory, and divides it into military farms at will and without rent upon condition of service at their own charge in arms whenever he commands them, it is the sword of an absolute monarchy.

4. If the nobility, being lords of the whole or of two parts in three of the whole territory, let their lands by good pennyworths to tenants at will or by their leases bound at their commands by whom they live to serve in arms upon pay, it is the sword of a regulated monarchy.

5. In countries that have no infantry or militia of free commoners, as in France and Poland, the nobility themselves are a vast body of horse [soldiers] and the sword of that monarchy.

6. If a people, where there neither is lord nor lords of the whole nor of two parts in three of the whole territory, for the common defense of their liberty and of their livelihood take their turns upon the guard or in arms, it is the sword of democracy.

7. There is a fourth kind of militia, or of men living more immediately by the sword, which are soldiers of fortune or a mercenary army.

8. Absolute monarchy must be very well provided with court guards or a mercenary army; otherwise, its military farmers having no bar from becoming proprietors the monarchy itself has no bar from changing into democracy.

Form of government (as to the military part) being thus completed is summed up in the three following Aphorisms:

9. In a regulated monarchy where there is an infantry, there needs not any mercenary army, and there the people live tolerably well.

10. In a regulated monarchy where there is no infantry, but the nobility themselves are a vast body of horse, there must also be a mercenary infantry, and there the people are peasants or slaves.

11. There is no such thing in nature as any monarchy (whether absolute or regulated) subsisting merely by a mercenary army, and without an infantry or cavalry planted upon the lands of the monarch or of his whole nobility.

VIII.   OF FORM IN THE LEGAL PART

1. If justice be not the interest of a government, the interest of that government will be its justice.

2. Let equity or justice be what it will, yet if a man be to judge or resolve in his own case, he resolves upon his own interest.

3. Every government, being not obnoxious [6] to any superior, resolves in her own case.

4. The ultimate result in every government is the law in that government.

5. In absolute monarchy the ultimate result is in the monarch.

6. In aristocracy or regulated monarchy the ultimate result is in the lords or peers, or not without them.

7. In democracy the ultimate result is in the people.

8. Law in absolute monarchy holds such a disproportion to natural equity as the interest of one man to the interest of all mankind.

9. Law in an aristocracy holds such a disproportion to natural equity as the interest of a few men to the interest of all mankind.

10. Law in democracy holds such a disproportion to natural equity as the interest of a nation to the interest of all mankind.

11. One government has much nearer approaches to natural equity than another, but in case natural equity and self-preservation come into competition, so natural is self-preserva-

[6] Harrington always uses the word "obnoxious" to mean "exposed to, liable to."

tion to every creature that in that case no one government has any more regard to natural equity than another.

12. A man may devote himself to death or destruction to save a nation, but no nation will devote itself to death or destruction to save mankind.

13. Machiavelli is decried for saying that "no consideration is to be had of what is just or unjust, of what is merciful or cruel, of what is honorable or ignominious, in case it be to save a state or to preserve liberty," which as to the manner of expression is crudely spoken. But to imagine that a nation will devote itself to death or destruction any more upon faith given or an engagement thereto tending than if there had been no such engagement made or faith given were not piety but folly.

14. Wheresoever the power of making law is, there only is the power of interpreting the law so made.

15. God, who has given His Law to the soul of that man who shall voluntarily receive it, is the only interpreter of His Law to that soul; such, at least, is the judgment of democracy. With absolute monarchy and with aristocracy, it is an innate maxim that the people are to be deceived in two things, their religion and their law; or that the Church or themselves are interpreters of all Scripture, as the priests were anciently of the Sibyls' Books.[7]

Form of government (as to the legal part) being thus completed is summed up in the three following Aphorisms:

16. Absolute monarchy (for the legal part of the form) consists of such laws as it pretends God has delivered or given the king and priests power to interpret, or it consists of such laws as the monarch shall [choose] or has chosen.

17. Aristocracy (for the legal part of the form) consists of

[7] The Sibyls', or Sibylline, Books were a collection of oracular pronouncements which were consulted by the Roman senate in times of crisis. Harrington is here concerned with the power which a priestly or political group can derive from the possession of, or the exclusive right to interpret, such scriptures.

such laws as the nobility shall choose or have chosen; or of such as the people shall choose or have chosen; provided they be agreed to by their lords, or by the king and their lords.

18. Democracy (for the legal part of the form) consists of such laws as the people, with the advice of their council or of the senate, shall choose or have chosen.

IX. OF FORM IN THE JUDICIAL PART

1. Multiplicity of laws, being a multiplicity of snares for the people, causes corruption of government.

2. Paucity of laws requires arbitrary power in courts or judicatories.

3. Arbitrary power (in reference to laws) is of three kinds: (1) in making, altering, abrogating, or interpreting of laws, which belong to the sovereign power; (2) in applying laws to cases which are never any one like another; (3) in reconciling the laws among themselves.

4. There is no difficulty at all in judging of any case whatsoever according to natural equity.

5. Arbitrary power makes any man a competent judge for his knowledge; but leaving him to his own interest, which oftentimes is contrary to justice, makes him also an incompetent judge in regard that he may be partial.

6. Partiality is the cause why laws pretend to abhor arbitrary power; nevertheless, seeing that not one case is altogether like another, there must in every judicatory be some arbitrary power.

7. Paucity of laws causes arbitrary power in applying them, and multiplicity of laws causes arbitrary power in reconciling and applying them too.

8. Arbitrary power, where it can do no wrong, does the greatest right, because no law can ever be so framed but that without arbitrary power it may do wrong.

9. Arbitrary power, going upon the interest of one or of a few, makes not a just judicatory.

10. Arbitrary power, going upon the interest of the whole people, makes a just judicatory.

11. All judicatories and laws which have been made by arbitrary power allow of the interpretation of arbitrary power and acknowledge an appeal from themselves to it.

12. That law which leaves the least arbitrary power to the judge or judicatory is the most perfect law.

13. Laws that are the fewest, plainest, and briefest leave the least arbitrary power to the judge or judicatory and, being a light to the people, make the most incorrupt government.

14. Laws that are perplex, intricate, tedious, and voluminous leave the greatest arbitrary power to the judge or judicatory and, raining snares on the people, make the most corrupt government.

15. Seeing no law can be so perfect as not to leave arbitrary power to the judicatory, that is the best constitution of a judicatory where arbitrary power can do the least hurt, and the worst constitution of a judicatory is where arbitrary power can do the most ill.

16. Arbitrary power in one judge does the most, in a few judges does less, and in a multitude of judges does the least hurt.

17. The ultimate appeal from all inferior judicatories is to some sovereign judge or judicatory.

18. The ultimate result in every government (as in absolute monarchy, the monarch; in aristocracy or aristocratical monarchy, the peers; in democracy, the popular assembly) is a sovereign judge or judicatory that is arbitrary.

19. Arbitrary power in judicatories is not such as makes no use of the law, but such by which there is a right use to be made of the laws.

20. That judicatory where the judge or judges are not obnoxious to partiality or private interest cannot make a wrong use of power.

21. That judicatory that cannot make a wrong use of power must make a right use of law.

22. Every judicatory consists of a judge or some judges

without a jury, or of a jury on the bench without any other judge or judges, or of a judge or judges on the bench with a jury at the bar.

Form of government (as to the judicial part) being thus completed, is summed up in the three following Aphorisms:

23. Absolute monarchy (for the judicial part of the form) admits not of any jury, but is of some such kind as a *cadee* or judge in a city, or as we say in a Hundred, with an appeal to a *cadaliskar* or a judge in a province, from whom also there lies an appeal to the *mufti,* who is at the devotion of the *grand signior* or of the monarch.

24. Aristocracy or aristocratical monarchy (for the judicial part of the form) may admit of a jury, so it be at the bar only, and consists of some such kind as delegates or ordinary judges, with an appeal to a house of peers or some such court as the *Parlement* at Paris, which was at the institution, in the reign of Hugh Capet, a parliament of sovereign princes.[8]

25. Democracy (for the judicial part of the form) is of some such kind as a jury on the bench in every Tribe, consisting of thirty persons or more annually eligible in one-third part by the people of that Tribe, with an appeal from thence to a judicatory residing in the capital city of the like constitution, annually eligible in one-third part out of the senate or the popular assembly or out of both, from which also there lies an appeal to the people; that is, to the popular assembly.

[8] Hugh Capet, founder of the continuing line of Capetian kings in France, was elected "king of the Aquitanians, of the Bretons, of the Danes [Normans], of the Goths, of the Spaniards and Gascons, and of the Gauls" in 987. As Harrington indicates, the monarchical power of Hugh was in fact slight: "Feudalism had, of course, in one way or another deprived the king of the actual exercise of any of [his] powers. It was the feudal noble who defended his own locality, maintained such law and order as there was, and administered such justice as could be had." Thompson and Johnson, *Introduction to Medieval Europe* (New York, 1937), p. 470.

X. OF THE ADMINISTRATION OF GOVERNMENT, OR REASON OF STATE

1. As the matter of a ship or of a house is one thing, the form of a ship or of a house is another thing, and the administration or reason of a ship or of the house is a third thing, so the matter of a government or of a state is one thing, the form of government or of a state is another, and the administration of a government (which is what is properly and truly called "reason of state") is a third thing.

2. There are those who can play and yet cannot pack the cards, and there are [those] who can pack the cards and yet cannot play.

3. Administration of government, or reason of state, to such as propose to themselves to play upon the square, is one thing; and to such as propose to themselves to pack the cards, is another.

4. Reason of state is that in a kingdom or a commonwealth which in a family is called "the main chance."

5. The master of a family that either keeps himself up to his ancient bounds or increases his stock looks very well to the main chance, at least if his play be upon the square; that is, upon his own abilities, or good fortune, or the laws; but if it were not upon the square, yet an estate, however gotten, is not for that a less estate in itself nor less descending by the law to his successors.

6. If a people, through their own industry or the prodigality of their lords, come to acquire liberty; if a few, by their industry or through the folly or slothfulness of the people, come to eat them out and make themselves lords; if one lord by his power or his virtue, or through their necessity, their wisdom, or their folly, can overtop the rest of these lords and make himself king, all this was fair play and upon the square.

7. Reason of state, if we speak of it as fair play, is foreign or domestic.

8. Reason of state which is foreign consists in balancing for-

eign princes and states in such a manner as you may gain upon them, or at least that they may not gain upon you.

9. Reason of state which is domestic is the administration of a government (being not usurped) according to the foundation and superstructures of the same if they be good, or so as not being good that they may be mended, or so as being good or bad they may be altered; or, the government being usurped, the reason of state then is the way and means whereby such usurpation may be made good or maintained.

10. Reason of state in a democracy which is rightly founded and rightly ordered is a thing of great facility, whether in a foreign or in a domestic relation. In a foreign, because one good democracy, weighing two or three of the greatest princes, will easily give the balance abroad at its pleasure; in a domestic, because it consists not of any more than giving such a stop in accumulation that the state comes not to be monarchical; which one reason of state being made good, all the rest goes well, and which one reason of state being neglected, all the rest comes in time to infallible ruin.

11. Reason of state in a democracy which is not right in its foundations may flourish abroad and be one, but at home will languish or be two reasons of state; that is, the reason of the state or orders of the nobility, which is to lord it over the people, and the reason of the popular state or order, which is to bring the commonwealth to equality; which two reasons of state, being irreconcilable, will exercise themselves against one another, first by disputes, then by plots, till it comes at last to open violence and so to the utter ruin of the commonwealth, as it happened in Rome.

12. Reason of state in an absolute monarchy (whether foreign or domestic) is but threefold, as first, to keep its military farmers or timariots to the first institution; next, to cut him that grows anything above his due stature or lifts up his head above the rest, by so much the shorter; and, last of all, to keep its arms in exercise.

13. In aristocratical monarchy, reason of state (as to the whole) is but one thing; that is, to preserve the counterpoise

of the king and the two, or the three, or the four estates; for in some countries, as in Poland, there are but two estates: the clergy and the nobility; in others, as in Sweden, there are four: the nobility, the gentry, the clergy, and the commons; in most others there are but three: the lords spiritual, the lords temporal, and the commons.

14. In aristocratical monarchy, reason of state (as to the parts) is a multifarious thing, every state having its peculiar reason of state, and the king also his reason of state; with the king, it is to balance the nobility, that he may hold them under; reason of state with the nobility is to balance the king, lest he should grow absolute; reason of state both with the king and the nobility is to keep down the people; and reason of state with the people is to drive at their liberty.

15. In forms that are pure, or in governments that have no more than an absolute prince or one state [i.e., estate] as absolute monarchy and equal or pure democracy, there is but one reason of state, and that is to preserve the form entire. In forms that are mixed (as in an inequal commonwealth where there are two estates, and in aristocratical monarchy where there is a king and two if not three estates), there are so many reasons of state to break the form that there has not been any inequal commonwealth which either the people have not brought to democracy or the nobility to monarchy. And scarce was there any aristocratical monarchy where (to omit the wars of the nobility with their king or among themselves) the people have not driven out their king, or where the king has not brought the people into slavery. Aristocratical monarchy is the true theater of expedient-mongers and state-empirics, or the deep waters wherein that Leviathan, the minister of state, takes his pastime.

16. The complaint that the wisdom of all these latter times in the affairs of princes consists rather in fine deliveries and shiftings of dangers or mischiefs when they are near than in solid and grounded courses to keep them off is a complaint in the streets of aristocratical monarchy and not to be remedied, because the nobility being not broken, the king is in

danger; and the nobility being broken, the monarchy is ruined.

17. An absurdity in the form of government (as that in a monarchy, there may be two monarchs) shoots out into a mischief in the administration or some wickedness in the reason of state, as in Romulus' killing of Remus, and the monstrous assassinations of the Roman emperors.

18. Usurpation of government is a surfeit that converts the best arts into the worst: *Nemo unquam imperium flagitio acquisitum bonis artibus exercuit.*[9]

19. As in the privation of virtue and in beggary, men are sharks or robbers, and the reason of their way of living is quite contrary to those of thrift, so in the privation of government, as in anarchy, oligarchy, or tyranny, that which is reason of state with them is directly opposite to that which is truly so, whence are all those black maxims set down by some politicians, particularly Machiavelli in his *Prince,* and which are condemned to the fire even by them who, if they lived otherwise, might blow their fingers.

20. Where the government from a true foundation rises up into proper superstructures or form, the reason of state is right and straight; but give our politician peace when you please, if your house stands awry, your props do not stand upright.

21. Take a juggler and commend his tricks never so much, yet if in doing so you show his tricks, you spoil him; which has been and is to be confessed of Machiavelli.

22. Corruption in government is to be read and considered in Machiavelli, as diseases in a man's body are to be read and considered in Hippocrates.

23. Neither Hippocrates nor Machiavelli introduced diseases into man's body nor corruption into government, which were before their times; and seeing they do but discover them, it must be confessed that so much as they have done tends not to the increase but the cure of them, which is the truth of these two authors.

[9] Literally, "no one who acquired empire by crime ever ran it well." Tacitus *History* i. 30.

THE COMMONWEALTH OF OCEANA
{Selections}

The title page of the first edition of 1656 carried the following quotation from Horace *Satires* i. 68ff.:

Tantalus a labris sitiens, fugientia captat Flumina: quid rides? mutato nomine, de te Fabula narratur.
[Tantalus, ever thirsty, catches at the streams that fly from his lips: why do you smile? but change the name and it is of you that the tale is told.]

THE COMMONWEALTH OF OCEANA

Part One of these selections consists of Harrington's Introduction to *The Commonwealth of Oceana* and the first two parts of that work, "The Preliminaries, Showing the Principles of Government," and "The Council of Legislators." Here Harrington, for the first time, explained the fundamental principles of his theory of politics and set the stage for the more detailed and elaborate "Model of the Commonwealth of Oceana." Virtually every important element of Harrington's theory is contained in the first two parts of the *Oceana;* in almost all of his subsequent writings, he was concerned either about making his style more popular, or providing his readers with further practical illustrations. This selection is found on pages B-54 of the first edition of *Oceana;* pages 9-61 of Liljegren's edition.

I

THE INTRODUCTION OR ORDER OF THE WORK

Oceana is saluted by the panegyrist after this manner: [1] "O the most blessed and fortunate of all countries, Oceana! How deservedly hath Nature with the bounties of Heaven and Earth endued thee, the ever-fruitful womb not closed with ice, nor dissolved by the raging star; where Ceres and Bacchus are perpetual twins. Thy woods are not the harbor of devouring beasts; nor thy continual verdure the ambush of serpents, but the food of innumerable herds and flocks presenting thee

[1] Harrington himself attributed the panegyric on England to Pliny the Younger. Liljegren, who notes that the passage is frequently quoted by English writers in the seventeenth century, is certain that neither of the Plinys had anything to do with it. For a full discussion, see his edition of *Oceana* (Liljegren), p. 230.

35

their shepherdess with distended dugs or golden fleeces. The wings of thy night involve thee not in the horror of darkness, but have still some white feather, and thy day is that for which we esteem life the longest." But this ecstasy of Pliny's, as is observed by Bertius,[2] seems to allude as well to Marpesia [Scotland] and Panopea [Ireland], now provinces of this commonwealth, as to Oceana herself.

To speak of the people in each of these countries, this of Oceana, for so soft a one, is the most martial in the whole world. "Let states that aim at greatness," says Verulamius,[3] "take heed how their nobility and gentlemen do multiply too fast, for that makes the common subject grow to be a peasant and base swain driven out of heart, and in effect but a gentleman's laborer. Even as you may see in coppice woods, if you leave the staddles [young trees] too thick you shall never have clean underwood, but shrubs and bushes; so in countries, if the gentlemen be too many, the commons will be base, and you will bring it to that, that not the hundredth pole will be fit for a helmet; especially as to the infantry, which is the nerve of an army, and so there will be great population and little strength. This which I speak of has been nowhere better seen than by comparing of Oceana and France, whereof Oceana though far less in territory and population has been nevertheless an overmatch: in regard the middle people of Oceana make good soldiers, which the peasants in France do not." In which words Verulamius (as Machiavelli has done before him) harps much upon a string which he has not perfectly tuned, and that is the *balance of dominion or property:* as it follows more plainly in his praise of "the profound and admirable device of Panurgus, King of Oceana [Henry VII,

---

2 Probably either Pierre Bertius (1565-1629), a professor of geography at Leyden, or Gaspar Barthius, annotator of an edition of Pliny's letters published at Jena in 1650. The reference, however, cannot be discovered in the works of either.

3 Verulamius was Harrington's name for Francis Bacon (1561-1626), who was Baron Verulam before he became Viscount St. Albans. The quotation is from his *Essay XXIX,* "Of the True Greatness of Kingdoms and Estates."

1457-1509]," in making farms and houses of husbandry of a standard; that is, maintained with such a proportion of land unto them as may breed a subject to live in convenient plenty and no servile condition, and to keep the plough in the hand of the owners, and not mere hirelings; and thus indeed (says he) you shall attain unto Virgil's character, which he gives of ancient Italy: *Terra potens armis atque ubere glebae!* [4]

But the tillage bringing up a good soldiery brings up a good commonwealth which [Bacon], in the praise of Panurgus, did not [understand], nor Panurgus in deserving that praise. For where the owner of the plough comes to have the sword, too, he will use it in defense of his own; whence it has happened that the people of Oceana, in proportion to their property, have been always free. And the genius of this nation has ever had some resemblance with that of ancient Italy, which was wholly addicted to commonwealths, and where Rome came to make the greatest account of her rustic tribes and to call her consuls from the plough. For, in the way of parliaments, which was the government of this realm, men of country lives have been still entrusted with the greatest affairs, and the people have constantly had an aversion from the ways of the court; ambition, loving to be gay and to fawn, has been a gallantry looked upon as having something in it of the livery and husbandry or the country way of life, though of a grosser spinning, as the best stuff of a commonwealth according to Aristotle *(Agricolarum democratica respublica optima)*,[5] such a one being the most obstinate assertress of her liberty and the least subject to innovation or turbulency. Wherefore till the foundations (as will be hereafter shown) were removed, this people was observed to be the least subject to shakings and turbulency of any. Whereas commonwealths upon which the city life has had the stronger influence, as Athens, have seldom or never been quiet, but at best are found to have injured their own business by overdoing it. Whence the urban

[4] "A land strong in arms and in the richness of the soil." *Aeneid* i. 531.
[5] See Aristotle *Politics* vi. 4. 1318b, 9. In Jowett's translation, ". . . the best material of democracy is an agricultural population."

tribes of Rome consisting of the *turba forensis*,[6] libertines that had received their freedom by manumission, were of no reputation in comparison of the rustics. It is true that with Venice it may seem to be otherwise, in regard the gentlemen (for so are all such called as have right unto that government) are wholly addicted to the city life; but then the *turba forensis*, the secretaries, *cittadini*, with the rest of the populace, are wholly excluded. Otherwise a commonwealth, consisting but of one city, would doubtless be stormy, in regard that ambition would be every man's trade; but where it consists of a country, the plough in the hands of the owner finds him a better calling and produces the most innocent and steady genius of a commonwealth, such as is that of Oceana.

Marpesia, being the northern part of the same island, is the dry nurse of a populous and hardy people, but [a country] where the staddles have been formerly too thick. Whence their courage answered not to their hardiness, except in the nobility, who governed that country much after the manner of Poland, save that the king was not elective, till the people received their liberty, the yoke of the nobility being broken by the commonwealth of Oceana, which in grateful return is thereby provided with an inexhaustible magazine of auxiliaries.

Panopea, the soft mother of a slothful and pusillanimous people, is a neighbor island anciently subjected by the arms of Oceana, since almost depopulated for shaking the yoke, and at length replanted with a new race. But (through what virtues of the soil or vices of the air soever it be) they come still to degenerate. Wherefore, seeing it is neither likely to yield men fit for arms nor necessary it should, it had been the interest of Oceana so to have disposed of this province, being both rich in the nature of the soil and full of commodious ports for trade, that it might have been ordered for the best in relation to her purse. Which in my opinion (if it had been thought upon in time) might have been best done by plant-

[6] The mob of the market place. Cicero *De republica* i. 17.28; Livy ix. 46.14.

ing it with Jews, allowing them their own rites and laws, for that would have brought them suddenly from all parts of the world and in sufficient numbers. And though the Jews be now altogether for merchandise, yet in the land of Canaan (since their exile from whence they have not been landlords) they were altogether for agriculture; and there is no cause why a man should doubt but, having a fruitful country and good ports, too, they would be good at both. Panopea, well-peopled, would be worth a matter of four millions dry rent; that is besides the advantage of the agriculture and trade which, with a nation of that industry, comes at least unto as much more. Wherefore Panopea, being farmed out unto the Jews and their heirs forever, for the pay of a provincial army to protect them during the term of seven years, and for two millions annual revenue from that time forward, besides the customs which would pay the provincial army, would have been a bargain of such advantage both to them and this commonwealth as is not to be found otherwise by either. To receive the Jews after any other manner into a commonwealth were to maim it; for they of all nations never incorporate, but taking up the room of a limb are of no use or office to the body, while they suck the nourishment which would sustain a natural and useful member.

If Panopea had been so disposed of, that knapsack, with the Marpesian auxiliary, had been an inestimable treasure; the situation of these countries being islands (as appears by Venice how advantageous such a one is to the like government) seems to have been designed by God for a commonwealth. And yet that [Venice], through the straitness of the place and the defect of proper arms, can be no more than a commonwealth for preservation; whereas this [Oceana] reduced to the like government is a commonwealth for increase, and upon the mightiest foundation that any has been laid from the beginning of the world unto this day.[7]

[7] For the distinction between commonwealths for preservation and those for increase, which Harrington took from Machiavelli, see p. 70.

Illam arcta capiens Neptunus compede stringit:
Hanc autem glaucis captus complectitur ulnis.[8]

The Sea gives law unto the growth of Venice, but the growth of Oceana gives law unto the Sea.

These countries, having been anciently distinct and hostile kingdoms, came by Morpheus the Marpesian [James, who ruled Scotland as James VI from 1566 to 1625 and England as James I from 1603 to 1625], who succeeded by hereditary right to the crown of Oceana, not only to be joined under one head, but to be cast, as it were, by a charm into that profound sleep which, broken at length by the trumpet of civil war, has produced those effects that have given the occasion to the ensuing Discourse, divided into four parts:

1. The *Preliminaries,* Showing the Principles of Government.

2. The *Council of Legislators,* Showing the Art of Making a Commonwealth.

3. The *Model* of the *Commonwealth of Oceana,* Showing the Effect of Such Art.

4. The *Corollary,* Showing Some Consequences of Such a Government.

THE PRELIMINARIES,
SHOWING THE PRINCIPLES OF GOVERNMENT

Gianotti,[1] the most excellent describer of the commonwealth of Venice, divides the whole series of government into two times or periods: the one ending with the liberty of Rome, which was the course or empire, as I may call it, of "ancient prudence," first discovered to mankind by God him-

---

8 "The one Neptune captures and binds with tight fetters:

He is captivated by the other and embraces her with his blue arms."

1 Donato Gianotti, the author of the *Libro de la republica de Venitiani* (Rome, 1542), was Harrington's major source of information (and occasionally misinformation) concerning the history of Venice and the Venetian Constitution.

self in the fabric of the commonwealth of Israel and afterward
picked out of his footsteps in nature and unanimously followed by the Greeks and Romans; the other beginning with
the arms of Caesar which, extinguishing liberty, were the
transition of ancient into "modern prudence," introduced by
those inundations of Huns, Goths, Vandals, Lombards, Saxons
which, breaking the Roman Empire, deformed the whole face
of the world with those ill features of government which at
this time are become far worse in these western parts, except
Venice (which escaping the hands of the barbarians by virtue
of her impregnable situation has had her eye fixed upon ancient prudence and is attained to a perfection even beyond her
copy).

Relation being had to these two times, government (to define it *de jure* or according to ancient prudence) is an art
whereby a civil society of men is instituted and preserved upon
the foundation of common right or interest, or (to follow
Aristotle and Livy) [2] it is the empire of laws and not of men.

And government (to define it *de facto* or according to modern prudence) is an art whereby some man, or some few men,
subject a city or a nation and rule it according to his or their
private interest, which, because the laws in such cases are
made according to the interest of a man, or of some few families, may be said to be the empire of men and not of laws.

The former is that kind which Machiavelli (whose books
are neglected) is the only politician that has gone about to re-
trieve, and that Hobbes (who would have his book imposed
upon the universities) [3] goes about to destroy. For "it is," says
Hobbes, "another error of Aristotle's *Politics* that in a well-
ordered commonwealth not men should govern, but the laws:
what man that has his natural senses, though he can neither
write nor read, does not find himself governed by them he fears

[2] Aristotle *Politics* iii. 16. 1287a and Livy ii. 1.1. The definition of
good government as government by laws rather than by men has been
a commonplace in Western political thought since the time of Aristotle.

[3] Hobbes, *Leviathan,* II, 30; in which Hobbes clearly expresses his
willingness to "undertake to teach the Universities."

and believes can kill or hurt him when he obeys not? Or, who believes that the law can hurt him, which is but words and paper, without the hands and swords of men?" [4] I confess that the magistrate upon his bench *(Magistratus est lex armata)* [5] is that unto the law which a gunner upon his platform is to his cannon. Nevertheless, I should not dare to argue with a man of any ingenuity after this manner: a whole army, though they can neither write nor read, are not afraid of a platform which they know is but earth or stone; nor of a cannon which without a hand to give fire to it is but cold iron; therefore, a whole army is afraid of one man. But of this kind is the ratiocination of Hobbes (as I shall show in divers places that come in my way) throughout his whole politics, or worse, as where he says of Aristotle and of Cicero, of the Greeks and of the Romans who lived under popular states, "that they derived those rights not from the principles of nature, but transcribed them into their books out of the practice of their own commonwealths, as grammarians describe the rules of language out of poets." [6] Which is as if a man should tell famous Harvey [7] that he transcribed his circulation of the blood not out of the principles of nature, but out of the anatomy of this or that body.

To go on, therefore, with this Preliminary Discourse: I shall divide it according to the two definitions of government relating to Gianotti's two times, into two parts: the first treating of the principles of government in general and according to the ancients, the second treating of the late governments of Oceana [England] in particular, and in that [treating] of modern prudence.

---

[4] *Ibid.*, IV, 46.

[5] "The magistrate is the law armed." Cf. Cicero *De legibus* iii. 2: "*Vereque dici potest magistratum legem esse loquentem, legem autem mutum magistratum.*"

[6] *Leviathan*, II, 21.

[7] William Harvey (1578-1657), the discoverer of the circulation of the blood, stood for Harrington as the outstanding example of the results to be achieved through use of the inductive, "scientific" method.

Government, according to the ancients and their learned disciple Machiavelli (the only politician of later ages), is of three kinds: the government of one man, or of the better sort, or of the whole people, which by their more learned names are called monarchy, aristocracy, and democracy. These they hold, through their proneness to degenerate, to be all evil. For, whereas they that govern should govern according to reason, if they govern according to passion they do that which they should not do. Wherefore, as reason and passion are two things, so government by reason is one thing and the corruption of government by passion is another thing; but not always another government, as a body that is alive is one thing, and a body that is dead is another thing, but not always another creature, though the corruption of one come at length unto the generation of another. The corruption, then, of monarchy is called tyranny; that of aristocracy, oligarchy; and that of democracy, anarchy. But legislators, having found these three governments at the best to be nought, have invented another consisting of a mixture of them all, which only is good. This is the doctrine of the ancients.

But Hobbes is positive that they are all deceived and that there is no other government in nature than one of the three; as also [he is positive] that the flesh of them cannot stink, the names of their corruptions being but the names of men's fancies; which will be understood when we are shown which of them was *Senatus populusque Romanus*.[8]

To go my own way and yet to follow the ancients, the principles of governments are twofold: internal, or the "goods of the mind"; and external, or the "goods of fortune." The goods of the mind are natural or acquired virtues, as wisdom, prudence, and courage, etc. The goods of fortune are riches. There be goods also of the body, as health, beauty, strength; but these are not to be brought to account upon this score, because if a man or an army acquire victory or empire it is more from their discipline, arms, and courage than from their natural health, beauty, or strength, [which is seen in

8 "The Senate and people of Rome"; i.e., the Roman Republic.

the fact] that a people conquered may have more of natural strength, beauty, and health, and yet find little remedy. The principles of government, then, are in the goods of the mind or in the goods of fortune. To the goods of the mind [corresponds] authority; to the goods of fortune, power or empire. Wherefore Hobbes, though he be right where he says that "Riches are Power," is mistaken where he says that "Prudence or the reputation of Prudence is power"; for the learning or prudence of a man is no more power than the learning or prudence of a book or author, which is properly authority.[9] A learned writer may have authority though he have no power, and a foolish magistrate may have power though he have otherwise no esteem or authority. The difference of these two is observed by Livy in *Evander,* of whom says he, *regebat magis Auctoritate quam Imperio* [he ruled rather by authority than power].[10]

To begin with riches, in regard that men are hung upon these not of choice as upon the other, but of necessity and by the teeth, for as much as he who wants bread is his servant that will feed him, if a man thus feed a whole people, they are under his empire.

Empire is of two kinds: domestic and national, or foreign and provincial.

Domestic empire is founded upon dominion.

Dominion is property, real or personal; that is to say, in lands or in money and goods.

Lands, or the parts and parcels of a territory, are held by the proprietor or proprietors, lord or lords of it, in some proportion; and such (except it be in a city that has little or no land and whose revenue is in trade) as is the proportion or balance of dominion or property in land, such is the nature of the empire.

If one man be sole landlord of a territory, or overbalance the people, for example, three parts in four, he is *Grand*

9 *Leviathan,* I, 10.
10 Livy i. 7.

Signior: for so the Turk is called from his property; and his empire is absolute monarchy.

If the few or a nobility, or a nobility with the clergy be landlords, or overbalance the people unto the like proportion, it makes the Gothic balance (to be shown at large in the second part of this Discourse), and the empire is mixed monarchy, as that of Spain, Poland, and late of Oceana.

And if the whole people be landlords, or hold the lands so divided among them that no one man or number of men within the compass of the few or aristocracy overbalance them, the empire (without the interposition of force) is a commonwealth.

If force be interposed in any of these three cases, it must either frame the government to the foundation, or the foundation to the government; or, holding the government not according to the balance, it is not natural but violent; and therefore, if it be at the devotion of a prince, it is tyranny; if at the devotion of the few, oligarchy; or if in the power of the people, anarchy. Each of which confusions, the balance standing otherwise, is but of short continuance, because [it is] against the nature of the balance which, not destroyed, destroys that which opposes it.

But there be certain other confusions which, being rooted in the balance, are of longer continuance and of greater horror. As first, where a nobility holds half the property, or about that proportion, and the people the other half; in which case, without altering the balance, there is no remedy but the one must eat out the other, as the people did the nobility in Athens, and the nobility the people in Rome. Secondly, when a prince holds about half the dominion and the people the other half, which was the case of the Roman emperors, planted partly upon their military colonies and partly upon the Senate and the people, the government becomes a very shambles both of the princes and the people. Somewhat of this nature are certain governments at this day which are said to subsist by confusion. In this case, to fix the balance is to entail misery; but, in the three former, not to fix it is to loose the government. Wherefore it being unlawful in Turkey that any should possess land but the Grand Signior, the balance is fixed by the law, and that empire firm. Nor, though kings often fell, was the throne of Oceana known to shake until the Statute of Alienations [11] broke the pillars by giving way to the nobility to sell their estates *(Si terra recedat, Jonium Aegaeo frangat mare)*.[12] Sparta, while she held unto her division of land made by Lycurgus, was immovable; but breaking that could stand no longer.[13] This kind of law fixing the balance in lands is called "Agrarian," and was first introduced by God himself, who divided the land of Canaan unto his people by lots, and is of such virtue that wherever it has held that government has not altered except by consent, as in that unparalleled example of the people of Israel when, being in liberty, they would needs choose a king.[14] But without an Agrarian, government, whether monarchical, aristocratical, or popular, has no long lease.

For dominion, personal or in money, it may now and then stir up a Melius or a Manlius [15] which, if the commonwealth be not provided with some kind of dictatorian power, may be dangerous, though it has been seldom or never successful: because unto property producing empire, it is required that it should have some certain root or foothold which, except in land, it cannot have, being otherwise, as it were, upon the wing.

Nevertheless, in such cities as subsist most by trade and have little or no land, as Holland and Genoa, the balance of treasure may be equal to that of land in the cases mentioned.

[11] Harrington here refers to the law, 4 Henry VII, c. 4, of 1489 entitled "An acte for the passing and transmutation of lands without fine." See p. 96.

[12] "If the land [i.e., Greece] should recede, the Ionian Sea would dash against the Aegean." Marcus Annaeus Lucanus *Pharsalia* i. 100f.

[13] Lycurgus, a semimythical Spartan lawgiver of the ninth century B.C., was one of Harrington's favorite examples of the advantages to be gained by the use of a single wise constitution-maker. His knowledge of Lycurgus was derived chiefly from Plutarch's *Lives*.

[14] I Sam. 8:5-7. See p. 117.

[15] For Melius and Manlius, see Livy iv. 13-16 and vi. 14-20.

But Hobbes, though he seems to scew at antiquity, following his furious master Carneades,[16] has caught hold of the public sword, to which he reduces all manner and matter of government, as where he affirms this opinion (that any monarch receives his power by covenant, that is to say, upon conditions) "to proceed from the not understanding the easy truth that covenants, being but words and breath, have no power to oblige, contain, constrain, or protect any man, [save] what they have from the public sword." [17] But, as he said of the law: that without this sword it is but paper, so might he have thought of this sword, that without a hand it is but cold iron. The hand which holds this sword is the militia of a nation, and the militia of a nation is either an army in the field or ready for the field upon occasion. But an army is a beast that has a great belly and must be fed; wherefore this will come unto what pastures you have, and what pastures you have will come unto the balance of property, without which the public sword is but a name or mere spit-frog. Wherefore, to set that which Hobbes says of arms and of contracts a little straighter, he that can graze this beast with the great belly as the Turk does his timariots may well deride him that imagines he received his power by covenant or is obliged unto any such toy: it being in *this* case only that covenants are but words and breath. But if the property of the nobility stocked with their tenants and retainers be the pasture of that beast, the ox knows his master's crib, and it is impossible for a king in such a constitution to reign otherwise than by covenant; or if he break it, it is words that come to blows.

"But," says Hobbes, "when an assembly of men is made sovereign, then no man imagineth any such covenant to have

[16] Carneades was a Skeptic philosopher of the second century B.C. He argued that men are governed solely by self-interest and that what is called justice is simply a rationalization for self-interest. Both Cicero in his *Republic* and Grotius in his *De jure belli ac pacis* (1625) chose to present their natural law theories in the form of an imaginary debate with Carneades.

[17] *Leviathan*, II, 18.

passed in the institution." [18] But what was that [made] by
Publicola, of appeal to the people, or that whereby the people had their tribunes? [19] "Fie," says he, "nobody is so dull
as to say that the people of Rome made a covenant with the
Romans to hold the sovereignty on such or such conditions,
which not performed, the Romans might depose the Roman
people." In which there are remarkable things, for, first, he
holds the commonwealth of Rome to have consisted of one
assembly, whereas it consisted of the Senate and the people;
that they were not upon covenant, whereas every law enacted
by them was a covenant between them; that the one assembly
was made sovereign, whereas the people who [alone] were
sovereign were such from the beginning, as appears by the
ancient style of their covenants or laws *(censuere Patres, jussit
Populus);* [20] that a council being made sovereign cannot be
made such upon conditions, whereas the Decemvirs,[21] being
a council that was made sovereign, was made such upon conditions; that all conditions or covenants making a sovereign,
the sovereign being made, are void, whence it must follow
that the Decemvirs being made were ever after the lawful
government of Rome, and that it was unlawful for the commonwealth of Rome to depose the Decemvirs; as also that
Cicero, if he wrote otherwise out of his commonwealth, did
not write out of nature. But to come unto others that see
more of this balance.

You have Aristotle full of it in divers places, especially

[18] *Loc. cit.*

[19] The first major step toward greater freedom for the plebeian class
came in 494 B.C. with the creation of the tribunes, who were empowered
to veto the acts of magistrates and to lay proposals before the plebeian
corporation; in 339 B.C. a Publilean Law provided that the agreement of
the Senate, previously required after a vote of the popular assembly,
must be given in advance, thus reducing it to a merely formal assent.

[20] "The Senate advised and the people voted." Livy x. 12.3.

[21] A commission of ten men appointed in 451 B.C. which codified the
laws of Rome in the famous Twelve Tables. When the *Decemviri* refused to retire at the completion of their task the plebeians seceded until,
in 449 B.C., the Valerio-Horatian Laws were passed, reaffirming the right
of appeal and the inviolability of the tribunes.

where he says that "immoderate wealth, as where one man or the few have greater possessions than equality or the frame of the commonwealth will bear, is an occasion of sedition which ends for the greater part in monarchy; and that for this cause the ostracism has been received in divers places, as in Argos and Athens. But that it were better to prevent the growth in the beginning than, when it has gotten head, to seek the remedy of such an evil." [22]

Machiavelli has missed it very narrowly and more dangerously for not fully perceiving that if a commonwealth be galled by the gentry, it is by their overbalance; he speaks of the gentry as hostile to popular governments, and of popular governments as hostile to the gentry. And [he seeks to make] us believe that the people in such [governments] are so enraged against them, that where they meet a gentleman they kill him, which can never be proved by any one example unless in civil war, seeing that even in Switzerland the gentry are not only safe, but in honor. But the balance as I have laid it down, though unseen by Machiavelli, is that which interprets him and that which he confirms by his judgment in many other as well as in this place, where he concludes

That he who will go about to make a commonwealth where there be many gentlemen, unless he first destroy them, undertakes an impossibility; and that he who goes about to introduce monarchy where the condition of the people is equal, shall never bring it to pass unless he cull out such of them as are the most turbulent and ambitious and make them gentlemen or noblemen, not in name but in effect; that is, by enriching them with lands, castles, and treasures that may gain them power among the rest and bring in the rest unto dependence upon themselves, to the end that they maintaining their ambition by the prince, the prince may maintain his power by them.[23]

Wherefore, as in this place, I agree with Machiavelli that a nobility or gentry overbalancing a popular government is the utter bane and destruction of it, so I shall show in another

[22] *Politics* v. 3. 1302b.
[23] *Discourses,* I, 55.

that a nobility or gentry in a popular government not over-balancing it is the very life and soul of it.[24]

By what has been said, it should seem that we may lay aside further disputes of the public sword, or of the right of the militia, which, be the government what it will or let it change how it can, is inseparable from the overbalance in dominion. Nor, if otherwise stated by the law or custom, as in the commonwealth of Rome (Consules sine lege Curiata rem militarem attingere non potuerunt)[25] where the people having the sword the nobility came to have the overbalance, avails it to other end than destruction. For, as a building swaying from the foundation must fall, so the law swaying from reason, and the militia from the balance of dominion [must also fall]. And so much for the balance of national or domestic empire which is in dominion.

The balance of foreign or provincial empire is of a contrary nature. A man may as well say that it is unlawful for him who has made a fair and honest purchase to have tenants, as for a government that has made a just progress and enlargement of itself to have provinces. But how a province may be justly acquired appertains to another place; in this I am to show no more than how or upon what kind of balance it is to be held, in order whereunto I shall first show upon what kind of balance it is not to be held. It has been said that national or independent empire, of what kind soever, is to be exercised by them that have the proper balance of dominion in the nation. Wherefore provincial or dependent empire is not to be exercised by them that have the balance of dominion in the province, because that would bring the government from provincial and dependent to national and independent. Absolute monarchy, as that of the Turks, neither plants her people at home nor abroad otherwise than as ten-

[24] See pp. 131-146.

[25] "Consuls, if they be not invested with the authority by a lex curiata, have no power to interfere in military affairs." Cicero's oration De lege agraria ii. 12.30.

ants for life or at will, wherefore her national and her provincial government is all one. But in governments that admit the citizen or subject unto dominion in lands, the richest are they that share most of the power at home. Whereas the richest among the provincials, though native subjects or citizens that have been transplanted, are least admitted to the government abroad; for men like flowers or roots being transplanted take after the soil wherein they grow. Wherefore the commonwealth of Rome, by planting colonies of her citizens within the bound of Italy, took the best way of propagating herself and naturalizing the country. Whereas if she had planted such colonies without the bounds of Italy, it would have alien'd [i.e., alienated] the citizens and given a root unto liberty abroad that might have sprung up foreign or savage and hostile to her. Wherefore she never made any such dispersion of her self and her strength till she was under the yoke of her emperors, who, disburdening themselves of the people as having less apprehension of what they could do abroad than at home, took a contrary course.

The Mamelukes [26] (which, till any man show me the contrary, I shall presume to have been a commonwealth consisting of an army, whereof the common soldier was the people, the commission officer, the senate, and the general, the prince) were foreigners, and by nation Circassians, that governed Egypt. Wherefore these never dared plant themselves upon dominion, which growing naturally up into the national interest must have dissolved the foreign yoke in that province.

The like may in some sort be said of Venice, the government whereof is usually mistaken. For Venice, though she do not take in the people, never excluded them. This commonwealth, the orders whereof are the most democratical or popular of all others in regard of the exquisite rotation of the senate, at the first institution took in the whole people; they that now live under the government without participation of it are

[26] The Mamelukes were a cavalry corps composed of former slaves who ruled Egypt from 1254 to 1811.

such as have since either voluntarily chosen so to do or were subdued by arms.[27] Wherefore the subject of Venice is governed by provinces, and the balance of dominion not standing, as has been said, with provincial government (as the Mamelukes dared not cast their government upon this balance in their provinces lest the national interest should have rooted out the foreign), so neither dare the Venetians take in their subjects upon this balance lest the foreign interest should root out the national (which is that of the three thousand now governing) and by diffusing the commonwealth throughout her territories lose the advantage of her situation, by which in a great part she subsists. And such also is the government of the Spaniard in the Indies, to which he deputes natives of his own country, not admitting the Creoles to the government of those provinces, though [they are] descended from Spaniards.

But if a prince or a commonwealth may hold a territory that is foreign in this [manner], it may be asked why he may not hold one that is native in the like manner? To which I answer, because he can hold a foreign by a native territory, but not a native by a foreign. And as hitherto I have shown what is *not* the provincial balance, so by this answer it may appear what it is, namely, the overbalance of a native territory to a foreign. For as one country balances itself by the distribution of property according to the proportion of the same, so one country overbalances another by advantage of divers kinds. For example, the commonwealth of Rome overbalanced her provinces by the *vigor* of a more excellent gov-

[27] Harrington argues that despite the fact that only a small fraction of the population was allowed to participate, the government of Venice was essentially democratic. The rigid restriction on participation began in 1297 with the closing of the membership of the Great Council, and Harrington argues that in effect those eligible for membership of the council *are* the real population of Venice. All other residents he simply classifies as foreigners, although by 1656 their families might have lived in Venice for more than three centuries. It is clear that Harrington's view was greatly influenced by Gianotti's account of Venetian history.

ernment opposed unto a crazier, or by a more exquisite militia opposed unto one inferior in courage or discipline; the like was that of the Mamelukes, being a hardy, unto the Egyptians that were a soft people. And the balance of a *situation* is in this kind of wonderful effect; [thus] the King of Denmark, being none of the most potent princes, is able at the Sound [28] to take toll of the greatest. And as this king by the advantage of the land can make the sea tributary, so Venice by the advantage of the sea, in whose arms she is impregnable, can make the land to feed her gulf. [As] for the colonies in the Indies [29], they are yet babes that cannot live without sucking the breasts of their mother cities, but such as I mistake if when they come of age they do not wean themselves: which causes me to wonder at princes that delight to be exhausted in that way. And so much for the principles of power whether national or provincial, domestic or foreign, being such as are external and founded in the goods of fortune.

I come to the principles of authority, which are internal and founded upon the goods of the mind. These the legislator that can unite in his government with those of fortune comes nearest to the work of God, whose government consists of heaven and earth. Which was said by Plato, though in different words, as, when princes should be philosophers, or philosophers princes, the world would be happy.[30] And, says Solomon, "There is an evil which I have seen under the Sun, which proceedeth from the ruler, *(enimvero neque nobilem neque ingenuum, nec libertinum quidem armis praeponere, regia utilitas est)* folly is set in great dignity and the rich (either in virtue and wisdom, in the goods of the mind, or those of fortune upon that balance which gives them a sense of the national interest [J.H.]) sit in low places. I have seen servants upon horses and princes walking as servants upon the

---

[28] The body of water between the North Sea and the Baltic Sea.
[29] By the "Indies" Harrington means America.
[30] Plato *Republic* v.

earth." [31] Sad complaints that the principles of power and of authority, the goods of the mind and of fortune, do not meet and twine in the wreath or crown of empire! Wherefore if we have anything of piety or of prudence, let us raise ourselves out of the mire of private interest, unto the contemplation of virtue, and put a hand unto the removal of "this evil from under the Sun"; this evil against which no government that is not secured can be good; this evil from which the government that is secure must be perfect. Solomon tells us that the cause of it is from the ruler, from those principles of power which, balanced upon earthly trash, exclude the heavenly treasures of virtue and that influence of it upon government which is authority. We have wandered the earth to find out the balance of power; but to find out that of authority we must ascend, as I said, nearer heaven, or to the image of God, which is the soul of man.

The soul of man (whose life or motion is perpetual contemplation or thought) is the mistress of two potent rivals, the one reason, the other passion, that are in continual suit. And according as she gives up her will to these or either of them is the felicity or misery which man partakes in this mortal life.

For as whatever was passion in the contemplation of a man, being brought forth by his will into action, is vice and the bondage of sin, so whatever was reason in the contemplation of man, being brought forth by his will into action, is virtue and freedom of soul.

Again, as those actions of a man that were sin acquire unto himself repentance or shame, and affect others with scorn or pity, so those actions of a man that are virtue acquire unto himself honor, and upon others *authority*.

Now government is no other than the soul of a city or na-

[31] The quotation from "Solomon" is from Eccles. 10:5-7. The Latin insert comes originally from Tacitus *Germania* 44, but Harrington's source (as indicated by his marginal note) was Grotius' *Annotationes in Vetus Testamentum* (Eccles. 10:7). It is quite clear that Harrington, having used the Biblical passage, consulted Grotius' annotation for supporting quotations.

tion. Wherefore that which was reason in the debate of a commonwealth, being brought forth by the result, must be virtue. And [in] as much as the soul of a city or nation is the sovereign power, her virtue must be law. But the government whose *law* is *virtue,* and whose *virtue* is *law,* is the same whose *empire* is *authority,* and whose *authority* is *empire.*

Again, if the liberty of a man consist in the empire of his reason, the absence whereof would betray him unto the bondage of his passions, then the liberty of a commonwealth consists in the empire of her laws, the absence whereof would betray her unto the lusts of tyrants. And these I conceive to be the principles upon which Aristotle and Livy (injuriously accused by Hobbes for not writing out of nature) have grounded their assertion that a "commonwealth is an empire of laws and not of men." But they must not carry it so. "For," says Hobbes—

the liberty whereof there is so frequent and honorable mention in the histories and philosophy of the ancient Greeks and Romans, and the writings and discourses of those that from them have received all their learning in the politics, is not the liberty of particular men, but the liberty of the commonwealth.[32]

He might as well have said that the estates of particular men in a commonwealth are not the riches of particular men but the riches of the commonwealth, for equality of estates causes equality of power, and equality of power is the liberty not only of the commonwealth but of every man. But surely a man would never be thus irreverent with the greatest authors and positive against all antiquity without some certain demonstration of truth; and what is it? Why—

there is written on the turrets of the city of Lucca in great characters at this day the word "Libertas," yet no man can thence infer that a particular man hath more liberty or immunity from the service of the commonwealth there than in Constantinople. Whether a commonwealth be monarchical or popular, the freedom is still the same.[33]

[32] *Leviathan,* II, 21.
[33] *Loc. cit.*

The mountain has brought forth, and we have a little equivo-
cation! For to say that a Lucchese has no more liberty or immunity *from* the laws of Lucca than a Turk has from those
of Constantinople, and to say that a Lucchese has no more
liberty or immunity *by* the laws of Lucca than a Turk has by
those of Constantinople, are pretty different speeches. The
first may be said of all governments alike, the second scarce of
any two, much less of these, seeing it is known that whereas
the greatest bashaw [34] is a tenant as well of his head as of his
estate at the will of his lord, the meanest Lucchese that has
land is a freeholder of both and not [meant] to be controlled
but by the law, and that framed by every private man to no
other end (or they may thank themselves) than to protect the
liberty of every private man, which by that means comes to
be the liberty of the commonwealth.

But seeing they that make the laws in commonwealths are
but men, the main question seems to be how a commonwealth
comes to be an empire of laws and not of men; or how the
debate or result of a commonwealth is so sure to be according
unto reason, seeing they who debate and they who resolve be
but men. "And as often as reason is against a man, so often
will a man be against reason." [35]

This is thought to be a shrewd saying, but will do no harm.
For be it so that reason is nothing but interest, there be divers
interests and so divers reasons.

As first, there is *private reason*, which is the interest of a
private man.

Secondly, there is *reason of state*, which is the interest (or
"error," as was said by Solomon) [36] of the ruler or rulers; that
is to say, of the prince, of the nobility, or of the people.

Thirdly, there is that reason which is *the interest of mankind* or of the whole. [Says Hooker:]

[34] Pasha.

[35] Hobbes, *Works*, III, 91 and IV, Epistle Dedicatory.

[36] The reference again is to Eccles. 10:5 (". . . like an error which proceedeth from a ruler.")

Now if we see even in those natural agents that want sense, that as in themselves they have a law which directs them in the means whereby they tend to their own perfection, so likewise that another law there is which touches them as they are sociable parts united into one body, a law which binds them each to serve unto others' good and all to prefer the good of the whole before whatsoever their own particular, as when stones or heavy things forsake their ordinary wont or center and fly upwards as if they heard themselves commanded to let go the good they privately wish and to relieve the present distress of nature in common.[37]

There is a common right, law of nature, or interest of the whole which is more excellent, and so acknowledged to be by the agents themselves, than the right or interest of the parts only. "Wherefore, though it may be truly said that the creatures are naturally carried forth to their proper utility or profit, that ought not to be taken in too general a sense, seeing divers of them abstain from their own profit either in regard of those of the same kind or at least of their young." [38]

Mankind, then, must either be less just than the creature or acknowledge also his common interest to be common right. And if reason be nothing else but interest, and the interest of mankind be the right interest, then the reason of mankind must be right reason. Now compute well, for if the *interest of popular government* come the nearest unto the *interest of mankind,* then the *reason of popular government* must come the nearest unto *right reason.*

But it may be said that the difficulty remains yet. For be the interest of popular government right reason, a man does not look upon reason as it is right or wrong in itself, but as it makes for him or against him. Wherefore, unless you can show such orders of a government as, like those of God in nature, shall be able to constrain this or that creature to shake off that inclination which is more peculiar to it and take up that

[37] Richard Hooker, *The Laws of Ecclesiastical Polity,* I, 3.5. Hooker (1586-1647) was the leading English exponent of the natural law tradition in political theory and deeply influenced John Locke's thought.

[38] Hugo Grotius (1583-1645), *De jure belli ac pacis,* Prolegomena.

which regards the common good or interest, all this is to no more end than to persuade every man in a popular government not to carve himself of that which he desires most, but to be mannerly at the public table and give the best from himself to decency and the common interest. But that such orders may be established as may, nay must, give the upper hand in all cases to the common right or interest, notwithstanding the nearness of that which sticks to every man in private, and this in a way of equal certainty and facility is known even to girls, being no other than those that are of common practice with them in divers cases. For example, two of them have a cake yet undivided which was given between them that each of them therefore may have that which is due. "Divide," says one to the other, "and I will choose, or let me divide, and you shall choose." If this be but once agreed upon, it is enough, for the divider dividing unequally loses in regard that the other takes the better half. Wherefore, she divides equally and so both have right. "O the depth of the wisdom of God!" and yet "by the mouths of babes and sucklings hath he set forth his strength." [39] That which great philosophers are disputing upon in vain is brought unto light by two silly girls, even the whole mystery of a commonwealth, which lies only in dividing and choosing. Nor has God (if his works in nature be understood) left so much to mankind to dispute upon, as who shall divide and who choose, but distributed them forever into two orders, whereof the one has the natural right of dividing and the other of choosing. For example:

A commonwealth is but a civil society of men. Let us take any number of men (as twenty) and forthwith make a commonwealth. Twenty men (if they be not all idiots, perhaps if they be) can never come so together but there will be such difference in them that about a third will be wiser, or at least less foolish than all the rest. These upon acquaintance, though it be but small, will be discovered and (as stags that have the

[39] Harrington here combines two Biblical quotations, the first from Rom. 11:33, the second from Ps. 8:2.

largest heads) lead the herd. For while the six discoursing
and arguing one with another show the eminence of their
parts, the fourteen discover things that they never thought on
or are cleared in divers truths which had formerly perplexed
them. Wherefore in matter of common concernment, difficulty, or danger, they hang upon their lips as children upon
their fathers' and the influence thus acquired by the six, the
eminence of whose parts is found to be a stay and comfort to
the fourteen, is *Authoritas Patrum,* the authority of the fathers. Wherefore this can be no other than a *natural aristocracy* diffused by God throughout the whole body of mankind
to this end and purpose. And, therefore, such as the people
have not only a natural, but a positive, obligation to make use
of as their guides, as where the people of Israel are commanded
to "take wise men and understanding and known among their
tribes, to be made rulers over them." [40] The six then approved
of, as in the present case, are the senate, not by hereditary
right or in regard of the greatness of their estates only, which
would tend to such power as might force or draw the people,
but by election for their excellent parts which tend to the
advancement of the influence of their *virtue* or *authority* that
leads the people. Wherefore the office of the senate is not to
be commanders, but counselors of the people. And that which
is proper unto counselors is, first, to debate the business whereupon they are to give advice and, afterward, to give advice in
the business whereupon they have debated. Whence the decrees of the senate are never laws, nor so called, but *Senatus
Consulta,* and these being maturely framed, it is their duty,
Ferre ad Populum, to propose in the case to the people.
Wherefore the senate is no more than the debate of the commonwealth. But to debate is to discern or put a difference between things that being alike are not the same, or it is sepa-
rating and weighing this reason against that, and that reason
against this, which is dividing.

The senate then having divided, who shall choose? Ask the
girls. For if she that divided must have chosen also, it had

40 Deut. 1:13.

been little worse for the other in case she had not divided at all but kept the whole cake to herself, in regard that, being to choose too, she divided accordingly. Wherefore if the senate have any further power than to divide, the commonwealth can never be equal. But in a commonwealth consisting of a single council, there is no other to choose than that which divided. Whence it is that such a council fails not to scramble, that is, to be factious, there being no other dividing of the cake in that case but among themselves.

Nor is there any remedy but to have another council to choose. The *wisdom* of the few may be the *light* of mankind, but the *interest* of the few is not the *profit* of mankind, nor of a commonwealth. Wherefore, seeing we have granted interest to be reason, they must not choose, lest it put out their light. But as the council dividing consists of the *wisdom* of the commonwealth, so the assembly or council choosing should consist of the *interest* of the commonwealth. As the wisdom of the commonwealth is in the aristocracy, so the interest of the commonwealth is in the whole body of the people. And whereas this, in case the commonwealth consist of a whole nation, is too unwieldy a body to be assembled, this council is to consist of such a representative as may be equal, and so constituted as can never contract any other interest than that of the whole people. The manner whereof being such as is best shown by exemplification, I remit to the model.[41] But in the present case, the six dividing and the fourteen choosing, must of necessity take in the whole interest of the twenty.

Dividing and choosing in the language of a commonwealth is debating and resolving, and whatsoever upon debate of the senate is proposed unto the people and resolved by them is enacted *Auctoritate Patrum Et Jussu Populi,* by the authority of the fathers and the power of the people, which concurring make a law.

But the law being made, says Hobbes, "is but words and

---

[41] By the "Model" Harrington means the second part of his *Commonwealth of Oceana,* which describes in detail the system of government which he proposed for England. See pp. 149-165.

paper without the hands and swords of men." Wherefore as those two orders of a commonwealth, namely the senate and the people, are *legislative,* so of necessity there must be a third to be *executive* of the laws made, and this is the magistracy; in which order with the rest being wrought up by art, the commonwealth consists of the senate proposing, the people resolving, and the magistracy executing. Whereby, partaking of the aristocracy as in the senate, of the democracy as in the people, and of monarchy as in the magistracy, it is complete. Now there being no other commonwealth but this in art or nature, it is no wonder if Machiavelli has showed us that the ancients held this only to be good.[42] But it seems strange to me that they should hold that there could be any other; for if there be such a thing as pure monarchy, yet that there should be such a one as pure aristocracy or pure democracy is not in my understanding. But the magistracy both in number and function is different in different commonwealths; nevertheless, there is one condition of it that must be the same in every one or it dissolves the commonwealth where it is wanting. And this is no less than that as the hand of the magistrate is the executive power of the law, so the head of the magistrate is answerable to the people that his execution be according to the law, by which Hobbes may see that the hand or sword that executes the law is *in* it and *not above* it.

Now whether I have rightly transcribed these principles of a commonwealth out of nature, I shall appeal unto God and to the world: unto God in the fabric of the commonwealth of Israel, and to the world in the universal series of ancient prudence. But in regard the same commonwealths will be opened at large in the Council of Legislators, I shall touch them for the present but slightly, beginning with that of Israel.

The commonwealth of Israel consisted of the senate, the people, and the magistracy. The people by their first division,

[42] *Discourses,* I, 2.

which was genealogical, were contained under thirteen tribes, houses, or families. Whereof the first born in each was prince of his tribe and had the leading of it (Num. 1), the tribe of Levi [alone] being set apart to serve at the altar had no other prince but the High Priest. In their second division they were divided locally by their Agrarian (Josh. 13-24) or the distribution of the land of Canaan to them by lot, the tithe of all remaining to Levi, whence according to their local division, the tribes are reckoned but twelve.

The assemblies of the people thus divided were methodically gathered by trumpets (Num. 10:7) unto the congregation, which was, it should seem, of two sorts. For if it were called by one trumpet only, the princes of the tribes and elders only assembled (Num. 10:4), but if it were called with two, the whole people gathered themselves into the congregation (Num. 10:3), for so it is rendered by the English. But in the Greek it is called *ecclesia,* or the Church of God (Judg. 20:2), and by the Talmudists, *Synagoga magna.* The word *ecclesia* was also anciently and properly used for the civil congregations or assemblies of the people in Athens, Lacedaemon, and Ephesus, where it is so called in Scripture (Acts 19:23), though it be rendered otherwise by the translators, not much as I conceive to their commendations seeing by that means they have lost us a good lesson, the Apostles borrowing that name for their spiritual congregations to the end that we might see they intended the government of the Church to be democratic or popular, as is also plain in the rest of their constitutions.

The Church or Congregation of the people of Israel assembled in a military manner (Judg. 20:2) and had the result of the commonwealth, or the power of confirming all their laws, though proposed even by God himself, as where they make him King (Exod. 19). And where they reject or depose him as civil magistrate and elect Saul (I Sam. 8:7), it is manifest that he gives no such example to a legislator in a popular government as to deny or evade the power of the people, which were a contradiction. But though he deservedly blamed the ingratitude of the people in that action, [he] commanded Samuel,

being next under himself supreme magistrate, "to harken unto
their voice," (for where the suffrage of the people goes for
nothing, it is no commonwealth) and comforted him saying,
"They have not rejected thee, but they have rejected me, that
I should not reign over them." [43] But to reject him that he
should not reign over them was as civil magistrate to depose
him. The power therefore which the people had to depose
even God himself as he was civil magistrate leaves little doubt
but that they had power to have rejected any of those laws
confirmed by them throughout the Scripture which, to omit
the several parcels, are generally contained (Deut. 29) under
two heads: those that were made by covenant with the people
in the land of Moab, and those which were made by covenant
with the people in Horeb; which two, I think, amount to
the whole body of the Israelite laws. But if all and every one
of the laws of Israel being proposed by God were no otherwise
enacted than by covenant with the people, then that only
which was resolved by the people of Israel was their law, and
so the result of that commonwealth was in the people. Nor
had the people the result only in matter of law, but the power
in some cases of judicature (Jos. 7:16; Judg. 20:8,9,10), as
also the right of levying war (Judg. 20:8,9,10; I Sam. 7:6,7,8),
cognizance in matter of religion (I Chron. 13:2; II Chron.
30:4), and the election of their magistrates, [such] as the judge
or dictator (Judg. 11), the king (I Sam. 10:17), the prince
(I Macc. 14). These functions were exercised by the *Synagoga
magna,* or Congregation of Israel, not always in one manner,
for sometimes they were performed by the suffrage of the people, *viva voce* (Exod. 9:3,4,5), sometimes by the lot only (Josh.
7; I Sam. 10), and all other [times] by the ballot or by a mixture of the lot with the suffrage as in the case of Eldad and
Medad, which I shall open with the senate.

The senate of Israel called in the Old Testament the "Seventy Elders," and in the New the *Sanhedrin* (which word is
usually translated the Council), was appointed by God and
consisted of seventy elders besides Moses (Num. 11), which

[43] I Sam. 8:7.

were at the first elected by the people (Deut. 1), but in what manner is rather intimated (Num. 11) than shown. Nevertheless, because I cannot otherwise understand the passage concerning Eldad and Medad, of whom it is said "that they were of them that were written, but went not up unto the Tabernacle," then with the Talmudists I conceive that Eldad and Medad had the suffrage of the tribes and so were written as competitors for magistracy. But coming afterwards to the lot, [they] failed of it, and therefore went not up into the Tabernacle, or place of confirmation by God, or to the session house of the senate with the seventy upon whom the lot fell to be senators. For the session house of the *Sanhedrin* was first in the Court of the Tabernacle and afterwards in that of the Temple where it came to be called the Stone Chamber or Pavement (John −). If this were the ballot of Israel, that of Venice is the same transposed. For in Venice the competitor is chosen, as it were, by lot, in regard that the electors are so made, and the magistrate is chosen by the suffrage of the Great Council or assembly of the people. But the *Sanhedrin* of Israel being thus constituted, Moses for his time, and after him his successor, sat in the midst of it as prince or archon, and at his left hand the orator or father of the senate; the rest of the bench, coming round with either horn like a crescent, had a scribe attending upon the tip of it.

This senate, in regard that the Legislator of Israel was infallible and the laws given by God such as were not fit to be altered by men, is much different in the exercise of their power from all other senates, except that of the Areopagites in Athens, which also was little more than a supreme judicatory. For it will hardly, as I conceive, be found that the *Sanhedrin* proposed to the people till the return of the Children of Israel out of captivity under Esdras; at which time there was a new law made, namely, for a kind of excommunication, or rather banishment, which had never been before in Israel. Nevertheless, it is not to be thought that the *Sanhedrin* had not always that right, which from the time of Esdras it more frequently exercised, of proposing unto the people, but [rather] that they forbore it in regard of the fullness and infallibility of the law already made, whereby it was needless. Wherefore the function of this council, which is very rare in a senate, was executive and consisted in the administration of the law made (Deut. 17:9,10,11). And whereas the council itself is often understood in Scripture by the priest and the Levite, there is no more in that save only that the priests and the Levites, who otherwise had no power at all, being in the younger years of this commonwealth, [as they were among] those that were best studied in the laws, were the most frequently elected into the *Sanhedrin*. For the courts consisting of three and twenty elders sitting in the gates of every city, and the triumvirates of judges constituted almost in every village, which were parts of the executive magistracy subordinate to the *Sanhedrin*, I shall take them at better leisure and in the larger discourse. But these being that part of this commonwealth which was instituted by Moses upon the advice of Jethro, the priest of Midian (Exodus 18), as I conceive a heathen, are to me a sufficient warrant even from God himself, who confirmed them, to make further use of human prudence wherever I find it bearing a testimony to itself, whether in heathen commonwealths or others. And the rather because so it is that we, who have the Holy Scriptures and in them the original of a commonwealth made by the same hand that made the world, are either altogether blind or negligent of it, while the heathens have all written theirs as if they had had no other copy. As, to be more brief in the present account of that which you shall have more at large hereafter:

Athens consisted of the Senate of the Bean proposing, of the church or assembly of the people resolving and too often debating, which was the ruin of it, as also of the senate of the Areopagites, the nine archons with divers other magistrates executing.

Sparta consisted of the Senate proposing, of the Church or congregation of the people resolving only and never debating, which was the long life of it, and of the two kings, the court of the ephors, with divers other magistrates executing.

Carthage consisted of the Senate proposing and sometimes resolving too, of the people resolving and sometimes debating too, for which fault she was reprehended by Aristotle, and she had her suffetes and her hundred men with other magistrates executing.

Rome consisted of the Senate proposing, the *Concio* or people resolving and too often debating, which caused her storms, as also of the *consuls, censors, aediles, tribunes, praetors, quaestors,* and other magistrates executing.

Venice consists of the Senate or *Pregati* proposing and sometimes resolving too, of the Great Council or assembly of the people in whom the result is constitutively, as also of the *Doge,* the *Signory,* the *Censors,* the *Dieci,* the *Quazancies,* and other magistrates executing.

The proceeding of the commonwealths of Switzerland and Holland is of a like nature, though after a more obscure manner. For the sovereignties, whether Cantons, Provinces, or Cities, which are the people, send their deputies commissioned and instructed by themselves (wherein they reserve the result in their own power) to the provincial or general convention or senate, where the deputies debate but have no other power of result than what was conferred upon them by the people or is further conferred by the same upon further occasion. And for the executive part they have magistrates or judges in every Canton, Province, or City, besides those which are more public and relate to the league, as for controversies between one Canton, Province, or City and another, or the like between such persons as are not of the same Canton, Province, or City.

But that we may observe a little further how the heathen politicians have written not only out of nature but, as it were, out of Scripture: as in the commonwealth of Israel, God is said to have been king, so the commonwealth where the law is king is said by Aristotle to be [the] kingdom of God.[44] And where by the lusts or passions of men a power is set above that of the law deriving from reason, which is the dic-

[44] *Politics* iii. 16. 1287a.

tate of God, God in that sense is rejected or deposed that he should not reign over them, as he was in Israel. And yet Hobbes will have it that

by reading of these Greek and Latin (he might as well in this sense have said Hebrew) authors, young men and all others that are unprovided of the antidote of solid reason, receiving a strong and delightful impression of the great exploits of war achieved by the conductors of their armies, receive withal a pleasing idea of all they have done besides and imagine their great prosperity not to have proceeded from the emulation of particular men, but from the virtue of their popular form of government, not considering the frequent seditions and civil wars produced by the imperfection of their policy.[45]

Where first the blame he lays to the heathen authors is in his sense laid to the Scripture, and whereas he holds them to be young men or men of no antidote that are of like opinions, it should seem that Machiavelli, the sole retriever of this ancient prudence, is to his solid reason a beardless boy that has newly read Livy. And how solid his reason is, may appear where he grants the great prosperity of ancient commonwealths, which is to give up the controversy. For such an effect must have some adequate cause, which to evade he insinuates that it was nothing else but the emulation of particular men, as if so great an emulation could have been generated without as great virtue, so great virtue without the best education, the best education without the best laws, or the best laws any otherwise than by the excellence of their policy.

But if some of these commonwealths, as being less perfect in their policy than others, have been more seditious, it is not more an argument of the infirmity of this or that commonwealth in particular than of the excellence of that kind of policy in general; if they that have not altogether reached [such a policy] have nevertheless had greater prosperity, what would befall them that should reach [it]?

In answer to which question let me invite Hobbes, who of all other governments gives the advantage to monarchy for

45 *Leviathan,* II, 29.

perfection, to a better disquisition of it by these three assertions:

The first: that the perfection of government lies on such a libration in the frame of it that no man or men in or under it can have the interest or, having the interest, can have the power to disturb it with sedition.

The second: that monarchy, reaching the perfection of the kind, reaches not to the perfection of government, but must have some dangerous flaw in it.

The third: that popular government, reaching the perfection of the kind, reaches the perfection of government and has no flaw in it.

The first assertion requires no proof.

For the proof of the second: monarchy, as has been shown, is of two kinds, the one by arms, the other by a nobility; and there is no other kind in art or nature. For if there have been anciently some governments called kingdoms, as one of the Goths in Spain and another of the Vandals in Africa, where the king ruled without a nobility and by a council of the people only, it is expressly said by the authors that mention them that the kings were but the captains and that the people not only gave them laws, but deposed them as often as they pleased. Nor is it possible in reason that it should be otherwise in like cases. Wherefore these were either no monarchies or had greater flaws in them than any other.

But for a monarchy by arms as that of the Turk (which of all models that ever were comes up to the perfection of the kind) it is not in the wit or power of man to cure it of this dangerous flaw, that the janizaries have frequent interest and perpetual power to raise sedition and to tear the magistrate, even the prince himself, in pieces. Therefore, the monarchy of Turkey is no perfect government.

And for a monarchy by a nobility as of late in Oceana (which of all other models before the declination of it came up to the perfection in that kind), it was not in the power or wit of man to cure it of that dangerous flaw that the nobility had frequent interest and perpetual power by their retainers and tenants to raise sedition and (whereas the janizaries occasion this kind of calamity no sooner than they make an end of it) to levy a lasting war unto the vast effusion of blood, and that even upon occasions wherein the people but for their dependence upon their lords had no concernment, as in the feud of the Red and White.[46] The like has been frequent in Spain, France, Germany, and other monarchies of this kind; wherefore monarchy by a nobility is no perfect government.

For the proof of the third assertion, Hobbes yields it to me that there is no other commonwealth but monarchical or popular; wherefore, if no monarchy be a perfect government, then either there is no perfect government or it must be popular, for which kind of constitution I have something more to say than Hobbes has said, or ever will be able to say, for monarchy; as:

1. That it is the government that was never conquered by any monarch, from the beginning of the world to this day; for if the commonwealths of Greece came under the yoke of the kings of Macedon, they were first broken by themselves.

2. That it is the government that has frequently led mighty monarchs in triumph.

3. That it is the government which, if it have been seditious, it has not been from any imperfection in the *kind,* but in the *particular constitution,* which, wherever the like has happened, must have been unequal.

4. That it is the government which, if it have been anything near equal, was never seditious; or let him show me what sedition has happened in Sparta or Venice.

5. That it is the government which, attaining to perfect equality, has such a libration in the frame of it that no man living can show which way any man or men in or under it can contract any such interest or power as

[46] Harrington refers, of course, to the Wars of the Roses (1455-1485) between the rival English houses of Lancaster (identified by a red rose) and York (identified by a white rose).

should be able to disturb the commonwealth with sedition; wherefore an equal commonwealth is that only which is without flaw and contains in it the full perfection of government.

But to return:

By what has been shown in *reason* and *experience* it may appear that, though commonwealths in general be governments of the senate proposing, the people resolving, and the magistracy executing, yet some are not so good at these orders as others, through some impediment or defect in the frame, balance, or capacity of them, according to which they are of divers kinds.

The first division of them is into such as are *single*, as Israel, Athens, Lacedaemon, etc., and such as are by *leagues*, as those of the Achaeans, Aetolians, Lyceans, Swiss, and Hollanders.

The second (being Machiavelli's) is into such as are for *preservation*, as Lacedaemon and Venice, and such as are for *increase*, as Athens and Rome, in which I can see no more than that the former take in no more citizens than are necessary for defense, and the latter so many as are capable of increase.

The third division (unseen hitherto) is into *equal* and *unequal*, and this is the main point especially as to domestic peace and tranquility. For to make a commonwealth unequal is to divide it into parties, which sets them at perpetual variance, the one party endeavoring to preserve their eminence and inequality, and the other to attain to equality. Whence the people of Rome derived their perpetual strife with the nobility or Senate. But in an *equal commonwealth* there can be no more strife than there can be overbalance in equal weights. Wherefore the commonwealth of Venice, being that which of all others is the most equal in the constitution, is that wherein there never happened any strife between the Senate and the people.

An equal commonwealth is such a one as is equal, both in the balance and foundation and in the superstructures; that is to say, in her Agrarian Law and in her rotation.

An *equal Agrarian* is a perpetual law establishing and preserving the balance of dominion by such a distribution that no one man or number of men within the compass of the few or aristocracy can come to overpower the whole people by their possessions in lands.

As the Agrarian answers to the foundation, so does rotation to the superstructures.

Equal rotation is equal vicissitude in government, or succession unto magistracy conferred for such convenient terms, enjoying equal vacations, as take in the whole body by parts succeeding others through the *free election* or suffrage of the people.

The contrary whereunto is prolongation of magistracy which, trashing the wheel of rotation, destroys the life or natural motion of a commonwealth.

The election or suffrage of the people is freest where it is made or given in such a manner that it can neither oblige *(qui beneficium accepit libertatem vendidit)* [47] nor disoblige another or, through fear of an enemy or bashfulness toward a friend, impair a man's liberty.

Wherefore says Cicero, "*Grata populo est tabella quae frontes aperit hominum, mentes tegit, datque eam libertatem ut quod velint faciant,*" [48] the tablet (or ballot of the people of Rome, who gave their votes by throwing tablets or little pieces of wood secretly into urns marked for the negative or affirmative) was a welcome constitution to the people, as that which, not impairing the assurance of their brows, increased the freedom of their judgment. I have not stood upon a more particular description of this ballot because that of Venice, exemplified in the Model, is of all others the most perfect.

An equal commonwealth (by that which has been said) *is a*

[47] "Who accepts a gift sells liberty." Cicero *De officiis* ii. 20.

[48] The full quotation, from Cicero's oration *Pro Plancio* iv. 16, reads: "For if the people cherishes its privilege of voting by ballot, which allows a man to wear a smooth brow while it cloaks the secrets of his heart, and which leaves him free to act as he chooses, while he gives any promise he may be asked to give, why do you insist that the courts should determine what a vote cannot?"

government established upon an equal Agrarian, arising into
the superstructures or three orders: the senate debating and
proposing, the people resolving, and the magistracy executing
by an equal rotation through the suffrage of the people given
by the ballot. For though rotation may be without the ballot,
and the ballot without rotation, yet the ballot not only as to
the ensuing Model includes both, but is by far the most equal
way; for which cause under the name of the ballot I shall
hereafter understand both that and rotation too.

Now having reasoned the principles of an equal commonwealth, I should come to give an instance of such a one in
experience if I could find it. But if this work be of any value,
it lies in that it is the first example of a commonwealth that
is perfectly equal. For Venice, though she come the nearest,
yet is a commonwealth for preservation, and such a one, considering the paucity of citizens taken in and the number not
taken in, is externally unequal. And though every commonwealth that holds provinces must in that regard be such, yet
not to that degree. Nevertheless, Venice internally and for her
capacity is by far the most equal, though she has not in my
judgment arrived at the full perfection of equality, both because her laws supplying the defect of an Agrarian are not so
clear nor effectual at the foundation, nor her superstructures
by the virtue of her ballot or rotation exactly librated, in regard that, through the paucity of her citizens, her greater
magistracies are continually wheeled through a few hands. As
is confessed by Gianotti [49] where he says that if a gentleman
come once to be *Savio di terra ferma,* it seldom happens that
he fails from thenceforth to be adorned with some one of the
greater magistracies, as *Savi di mare, Savi di terra ferma, Savi
Grandi,* Counselors, those of the decemvirate or dictatorian
council, the *Aurogatori* or censors which require no vacation
or interval. Wherefore, if this in Venice or that in Lacedaemon, where the kings were hereditary and the senators (though
elected by the people) for life, cause no inequality (which is
hard to be conceived) in a commonwealth for preservation or

[49] Gianotti, *op. cit.,* p. 73 (1548 ed.).

such a one as consists of a few citizens, yet is it manifest that it would cause a very great one in a commonwealth for increase or consisting of the many, which by the engrossing [of] the magistracies in a few hands would be obstructed in their rotation.

But there be [those] that say (and think it a strong objection), let a commonwealth be as equal as you can imagine, two or three men when all is done will govern it; and there is that in it which, notwithstanding the pretended sufficiency of a popular state, amounts to a plain confession of the imbecility of that policy and of the prerogative of monarchy, for as much as popular governments in difficult cases have had recourse to dictatorian power as in Rome.

To which I answer, that as truth is a spark whereunto objections are like bellows, so in this our commonwealth shines. For the eminence acquired by suffrage of the people in a commonwealth, especially if it be *popular* and *equal,* can be ascended by no other steps than the universal acknowledgment of virtue; and where men excel in virtue, the commonwealth is stupid and unjust if accordingly they do not excel in authority. Wherefore this is both the advantage of virtue, which has her due encouragement, and the commonwealth, which has her due services. These are the philosophers which Plato would have to be princes, the princes which Solomon would have to be mounted, and their steeds are those of *authority,* not *empire.* Or, if they be buckled to the chariot of empire, as that of the dictatorian power, like the chariot of the sun it is glorious for terms and vacations or intervals. And as a commonwealth is a government of *laws* and not of *men,* so is this the principality of the virtue and not of the man. If that fail or set in one, it rises in another, which is created his immediate successor.

> . . . *Uno avulso non deficit alter,*
> *Aureus, et simili frondescit virga metallo.*[50]

[50] "And when [a bough] is torn away, another gold one grows in its place with leaves of the same metal." The Sibyl is describing Proserpina's tree to Aeneas. Virgil *Aeneid* vi. 143f.

And this takes away that vanity from under the sun which is an error proceeding more or less from all other rulers under heaven but an equal commonwealth.

These things considered, it will be convenient in this place to speak a word to such as go about to insinuate to the nobility or gentry a fear of the people, or into the people a fear of the nobility or gentry, as if their interests were each destructive to [the] other, when in truth an army may as well consist of soldiers without officers or of officers without soldiers, as a commonwealth, especially such a one as is capable of greatness, of a people without a gentry or of a gentry without a people. Wherefore this (though not always so intended, as may appear by Machiavelli [51] who else would be guilty) is a pernicious error. There is something first in the making of a commonwealth, then in the governing of her, and last of all in the leading of her armies, which, though there be great divines, great lawyers, great men in all professions, seems to be peculiar to the genius of a gentleman. For so it is in the universal series of [history], that if any man have founded a commonwealth, he was first a gentleman. Moses had his education by the daughter of Pharaoh; Theseus and Solon, of noble birth, were held by the Athenians worthy to be kings; Lycurgus was of the blood-royal; Romulus and Numa princes; Brutus and Publicola patricians; the Gracchi that lost their lives for the people of Rome and the restitution of that commonwealth were the sons of a father adorned with two Triumphs, and of Cornelia, the daughter of Scipio, who being sought in marriage by King Ptolemy, disdained to be the queen of Egypt. And the most renowned Olphaus Megaletor,[52] sole Legislator (as you will see) of the Commonwealth of Oceana, was derived from a noble family. Nor will it be any occasion of scruple

---

[51] Cf. *Discourses*, I, 55. Harrington, who admired Machiavelli greatly, was unwilling to admit that this passage meant what it seems to mean.

[52] Olphaus Megaletor was Harrington's name for Oliver Cromwell, probably derived from the Greek words "whole" and "light" plus "great" and "heart." Cromwell, in a speech on September 12, 1654, said, "I was by birth a gentleman."

in this case that Hobbes affirms the politics to be no ancienter than his book *De cive*. Such also as have gotten any fame in the civil government of a commonwealth, or by the leading of her armies, have been gentlemen. For so in all other respects were those plebeian magistrates elected by the people of Rome, being of known descents and of equal virtues, save only that they were excluded from the name by the usurpation of the patricians. Holland, through this defect at home, has borrowed princes for her generals and gentlemen for her commanders, of divers nations. And Switzerland, if she have defect in this kind, rather lends her people to the colors of other princes than makes that noble use of them herself which should assert the liberty of mankind. For where there is not a nobility to bolt out the people, they are slothful, regardless of the world and the public interest of liberty, as even that of Rome had been without her gentry. Wherefore let the people embrace the gentry in peace as the light of their eyes and in war as the trophy of their arms. And if Cornelia disdained to be Queen of Egypt, if a Roman consul looked down from his tribunal upon the greatest king, let the nobility love and cherish the people that afford them a throne so much higher in a commonwealth, and in the acknowledgment of their virtue, than the crowns of monarchs.

But if the equality of a commonwealth consists in the equality first of the Agrarian and next of the rotation, then the inequality of a commonwealth must consist in the absence or inequality of the Agrarian or of the rotation, or of both.

Israel and Lacedaemon, which commonwealths (as the people of [the latter], in [the history of] Josephus,[53] claim [to be] kindred of [the former]) have great resemblance, were each of them equal in their Agrarian and unequal in their rotation, especially Israel, where the *Sanhedrin* or senate first elected by the people, as appears by the words of Moses, took upon them [selves] thenceforth, without any precept of God, to substitute their successors by ordination; which having been there of *civil* use, as excommunication, community of

---

[53] Josephus *Antiquitatum Judaicarum* xii. 4.10.

goods, and other customs of the Essenes (who were many of them converted) came afterwards to be introduced into the Christian Church. And the election of the judge, *suffes,* or dictator was irregular both for the occasion, the term, and the vacation of that magistracy, as you find in the Book of Judges, where it is often repeated that in those days there was no king in Israel, that is, no judge; and in the first of Samuel, where Ely judged Israel forty years, and Samuel all his life. In Lacedaemon, the election of the senate being by suffrage of the people, though for life, was not altogether so unequal, but the hereditary right of kings, but for the Agrarian, [would] have ruined her.

Athens and Rome were unequal as to their Agrarian, that of Athens being infirm and that of Rome none at all; for if it were more anciently carried, it was never kept. Whence by the time of Tiberius Gracchus the nobility had almost eaten the people quite out of their lands, which they held in the occupation of tenants and servants. Whereupon the remedy being too late and too vehemently applied, that commonwealth was ruined.

These also were unequal in their rotation, but in a contrary manner: Athens, in regard that the senate, chosen at once by lot, not by suffrage, and changed every year not in part, but the whole, consisted not of the natural aristocracy nor [sat] long enough to understand or be perfect in their office, had sufficient authority to withhold the people from that perpetual turbulence in the way which was ruin in the end, in spite of Nicias, who did what a man could do to help it. But as Athens [fell] by the headiness of the people, so Rome fell by the ambition of the nobility, through the want of an equal rotation which, if the people had [been admitted] into the Senate and timely into the magistracies—whereof the former was always usurped by the patricians and latter [too] for the most part—they had both carried and held their Agrarian, and that [would] have rendered that commonwealth immovable.

But let a commonwealth be equal or unequal, it must consist, as has been shown by reason and all experience, of the three general orders; that is to say, *of the senate debating and proposing, of the people resolving, and of the magistracy executing.* Wherefore I can never wonder enough at Hobbes, who, without any reason or example, will have it that a commonwealth consists of a single person or of a single assembly, nor sufficiently pity that "a thousand gentlemen, whose minds otherwise would have wavered, he has framed (as is affirmed by himself) unto a conscientious obedience (for so he is pleased to call it) of such a government." [54]

But to finish this part of the discourse, which I intend for as complete an epitome of ancient prudence and, in that, of the whole art of the politics as I am able to frame in so short a time:

The first two orders, that is to say, the senate and the people, are *legislative,* whereunto answers that part of this science which by politicians is entitled *De legibus* or of laws. And the third order is *executive,* to which answers that part of the same science which is styled *De judiciis,* or of the frame and course of courts or judicatories. A word to each of these will be necessary.

And first for laws: they are either ecclesiastical or civil, such as concern religion or government. (Somebody blushes, but I will do no harm.)

Ecclesiastical laws or such as concern religion, according to the universal course of ancient prudence, are in the power of the magistrate; but according to the common practice of modern prudence, since the papacy, torn out of his hands.

But as a government pretending to liberty and suppressing the liberty of conscience, which (because religion not according to a man's conscience can as to him be none at all) is the main [form of liberty], must be a contradiction, so a man that, pleading for the liberty of private conscience, refuses liberty to the national conscience must be absurd.

[54] "[My doctrine] hath framed the minds of a thousand gentlemen to a conscientious obedience to the present government which otherwise would have wavered in that point." Hobbes, *Works,* VII, 335f.

Now a commonwealth is nothing else but the national conscience. And if the conviction of a man's private conscience produce his private religion, the conviction of the national conscience must produce a national religion. Whether this be well reasoned, as also whether these two may stand together, will best be shown by the examples of the ancient commonwealths taken in their order.

In that of Israel, the government of the national religion appertained not to the priests and Levites otherwise than as [they happened] to [be members of] the *Sanhedrin* or senate, to which they had no right at all but by election. It is in this capacity, therefore, that the people are commanded under pain of death, "to hearken unto them, and to do according to the sentence of the law which they should teach." [55] But in Israel the law ecclesiastical and civil was the same; therefore the *Sanhedrin* having the power of one had the power of both. But as the national religion appertained to the jurisdiction of the *Sanhedrin,* so the liberty of conscience appertained from the same date and by the same right to the prophets and their disciples; as where it is said, "I will raise up a prophet—and whosoever will not hearken unto my words which he shall speak in my Name, I will require it of him." [56] Which words relate to prophetic right, which was above all the orders of this commonwealth; whence Elijah not only refused to obey the king, but destroyed his messengers with fire.[57] And whereas it was not lawful by the national religion to sacrifice in any other place than the Temple, a prophet was his own temple and might sacrifice where he would, as Elijah did in Mount Carmel.[58] By this right John the Baptist and our Saviour, to whom it more particularly related, had their disciples and taught the people; whence is derived our present right of *gathered congregations.* Wherefore the Christian religion grew up according to the orders

[55] Deut. 17:9ff.
[56] Deut. 18:18ff.
[57] II Kings, 1:9ff.
[58] I Kings, 18:19ff.

of the commonwealth of Israel and not against them. Nor was the liberty of conscience infringed by this government till the civil liberty of the same was lost, as under Herod, Pilate, and Tiberius, a three-piled tyranny.

To proceed, Athens preserved her religion, by the testimony of Paul,[59] with great superstition. If Alcibiades, that atheistical fellow, had not showed them a fair pair of heels they [would] have shaved off his head for shaving their Mercuries and making their gods look ridiculously upon them without beards. Nevertheless, if Paul reasoned with them, they loved news, for which he was the more welcome; and if he converted Dionysius the Areopagite, that is, one of the senators, there followed neither any hurt to him nor loss of honor to Dionysius. And for Rome, if Cicero in his most excellent book, *De natura deorum,* overthrew the national religion of that commonwealth, he was never the farther from being consul. But there is a meanness and poorness in modern prudence not only unto the damage of civil government, but of religion itself. [For to make a man in matter of religion, which admits not of sensible demonstration, *(jurare in verba magistri)*[60] engage to believe no otherwise than is believed by my Lord Bishop or Goodman Presbyter is a pedantism that has made the sword to be a rod in the hands of schoolmasters, by which means,][61] whereas Christian religion is the farthest of any from countenancing war, there never was a war of religion but since Christianity. For which we are beholden to the Pope, for the Pope not giving liberty of conscience to princes and commonwealths, they cannot give that to their subjects which they have not. Whence both princes and subjects either

[59] Acts 17:15ff.

[60] "To swear as any master dictates." See Horace *Epistles* i. 1.14.

[61] The passage in brackets appears in Liljegren's edition of the *Oceana* (page 38) based on copies of the first edition in the Royal Library at Copenhagen and in the British Museum. It does not, however, appear in the copy of the same edition from which the present selections have been taken. Apparently there are only four passages in which differences occur, and all of these are minor. Both Liljegren's editions and the one used here were printed for D. Pakeman in London in 1656.

through his instigation or disputes among themselves have introduced that execrable custom, never known in the world before, of fighting for religion and denying the magistrate to have any jurisdiction of it. Whereas the magistrates, losing the power of religion, lose the liberty of conscience, which [in that case] has nothing to protect it. Wherefore, if the people be otherwise taught, it concerns them to look about them and distinguish between the shrieking of the lapwing and the voice of the turtle.

To come to civil laws, if they stand one way and the balance another, it is the case of a government which of necessity must be new modeled. Wherefore the lawyers advising you upon like occasions to fit the government to their laws are no more to be regarded than your tailor if he should desire you to fit your body to his doublet. There is also danger in the plausible pretense of reforming the law, except the government be good, in which case it is a good tree and [trouble not yourselves overmuch] [62] brings not forth evil fruit. Otherwise, if the tree be evil, you can never reform the fruit. [Or if a root that is naught bring forth fruit of this kind that seems to be good, take the more heed, for it is the ranker poison. It was nowise probable if Augustus had not made excellent laws that the bowels of Rome could have come to be so miserably eaten out by the tyranny of Tiberius and his successors.] [63] Begin with reformation of the government by the laws, but first begin with reformation of the laws by the government. The best rule as to the laws in general is that they be few. Rome by the testimony of Cicero was best governed under those of the Twelve Tables; and by the testimony of Tacitus, *"Plurimae leges, corruptissima respublica."* [64] You will be told that where the laws be few they leave much to arbitrary power; but where they be many they leave more;

[62] See note 61.

[63] See note 61.

[64] For Cicero, see *De legibus* ii. 7-10; for Tacitus' opinion that "the more numerous the laws, the more corrupt the republic," see *Annales* iii. 27.

the laws in that case, according to Justinian and the best lawyers, being as litigious as the suitors. Solon made few, Lycurgus fewer, laws; commonwealths have fewest at this day of all other governments. And to conclude this part with a word *de judiciis,* or the constitution or course of courts: it is such in Venice as the arbitrary power of them can never retard or do hurt to business, but produces the quickest dispatch and the most righteous dictates of justice that are perhaps in human nature.[65] The manner of them I shall not stand in this place to describe, because it is exemplified at large in the judicature of the people of Oceana. And thus much of ancient prudence, and the first branch of this Preliminary Discourse.

THE SECOND PART OF THE PRELIMINARIES

In the second part I shall endeavor to show the rise, progress, and declination of modern prudence.

The date of this kind of policy is to be computed, as was shown, from those inundations of Goths, Vandals, Huns, and Lombards that overwhelmed the Roman Empire.[66] But as there is no appearance in the bulk or constitution of modern prudence that she should ever have been able to come up and grapple with the ancient, so something of necessity must have interposed whereby this came to be enervated and that to receive strength and encouragement. And this was the exe-

[65] The alternative reading of this sentence in Liljegren's edition is: "And to conclude this part with a word *de judiciis,* or of the constitution or course of courts: it is a discourse not otherwise capable of being well managed but by particular examples, both the constitution and course of courts being divers in different governments, but best beyond compare in Venice, where they regard not so much the arbitrary power of their courts as the constitution of tnem; whereby that arbitrary power being altogether unable to retard or do hurt unto business, produces and must produce the quickest dispatch and the most righteous dictates of justice that are perhaps in human nature."

[66] Harrington here refers to the invasions of the West during the fourth and fifth centuries A.D.

crable reign of the Roman Emperors taking rise from (that *felix scelus*) [67] the arms of Caesar, in which storm the ship of the Roman commonwealth was forced to disburden herself of that precious freight which never since could emerge or raise the head but in the Gulf of Venice.

It is said in Scripture, "Thy evil is of thyself, O Israel!" To which answers that of the moralists, *"Nemo nocetur nisi ex se,"* as also the whole matter of the politics. At present this example of the Romans who, through a negligence committed in their agrarian laws, let in the sink of luxury and forfeited the inestimable treasure of liberty for themselves and posterity.

Their agrarian laws were such whereby their lands ought to have been divided among the people either without mention of a colony, in which case they were not obliged to change their abode, or with mention and upon condition of a colony, in which case they were to change their abode and, leaving the city, to plant themselves upon the lands so assigned. The lands assigned, or that ought to have been assigned, in either of these ways were of three kinds: such as were taken from the enemy and distributed to the people; or such as were taken from the enemy and under color of being reserved to the public use were by stealth possessed by the nobility; or such as were bought with the public money to be distributed. Of the laws offered in these cases, those which divided the lands taken from the enemy or purchased with the public money never occasioned any dispute. But such as drove at dispossessing the nobility of their usurpations and dividing the common purchase of the sword among the people were never touched but they caused earthquakes, nor could ever be obtained by the people; or being obtained, be observed by the nobility, who not only preserved their prey but, growing vastly rich upon it, bought the people by degrees quite out of those shares that had been conferred upon them. This the Gracchi coming too late to perceive, found the balance of the commonwealth to be lost. But putting the people (when they

[67] Literally, "that happy crime."

had least force) by forcible means unto the recovery of it did ill, seeing it neither could nor did tend to any more than to show them by worse effects that what the wisdom of their leaders had discovered was true. For (quite contrary to what has happened in Oceana where, the balance falling to the people, they have overthrown the nobility) the nobility of Rome under the conduct of Sylla [68] overthrew the people and the commonwealth. Seeing Sylla first introduced that new balance which was the foundation of the succeeding monarchy in the plantation of military colonies, instituted by his distribution of the conquered lands not now of enemies but of citizens to forty-seven legions of his soldiers, so that how he came to be *dictator perpetuus* or other magistrates to succeed him in like power is no miracle.

These military colonies, in which manner succeeding emperors continued (as Augustus by the distribution of the veterans whereby he had overcome Brutus and Cassius) to plant their soldiery, consisted of such as I conceive were they that are called *milites beneficiarii,* in regard that the tenure of their lands was by way of *benefices,* that is, for life, and upon condition of duty or service in the war upon their own charge. These *benefices* Alexander Severus granted to the heirs of the incumbents but on the same conditions. And such was the dominion by which the Roman emperors gave their balance. But to the *beneficiaries,* as was no less than necessary for the safety of the prince, a matter of eight thousand by the example of Augustus were added which departed not from his sides, but were his perpetual guard, called pretorian bands. Though these, according to the incurable flaw already observed in this kind of government, became the most frequent butchers of their lords that are to be found in [history]. Thus far the Roman monarchy is so much the same with that at this day in Turkey, consisting of a camp and a horse-quarter, a camp in regard of her spahies and janizaries, the perpetual guard of the prince except they also chance to be liquorish

[68] Lucius Cornelius Sulla (138-78 B.C.), Roman general, proconsul and dictator (83-79 B.C.).

after his blood, and a horse-quarter in regard of the distribution of his whole land unto tenants for life upon condition of continual service, or as often as they shall be commanded at their own charge by "timars," being a word which they say signifies *benefices,* that it shall save me a labor of opening the government.

But the fame of Mohammed and his prudence is especially founded in this: that whereas the Roman monarchy (except that of Israel) was the most imperfect, the Turkish is the most perfect that ever was. Which happened in that the Roman (as the Israelite of the *Sanhedrin* and the Congregation) had a mixture of the senate and the people, and the Turkish is pure; and that this was pure and the other mixed happened not through the wisdom of the legislators, but the different genius of the nations, the people of the Eastern parts, except the Israelites (which is to be attributed to their Agrarian) having been such as scarce ever knew any other condition than that of slavery. And these of the Western having ever had such a relish of liberty, as through what despair soever could never be brought to stand still while the yoke was putting on their necks, but by being fed with some hopes of reserving to themselves some part of their freedom.

Wherefore Julius Caesar (says Suetonius, *comitia cum populo sortitus est*)[69] contented himself in naming half the magistrates, to leave the rest to the suffrage of the people. And Maecenas, though he would not have Augustus to give the people their liberty, would not have him take it away; for says he, *"Neque id existimare debes autorem me tibi esse, ut tyrannidem in S. P. Q. R. in servitutem redactum teneas: quod neque dicere meum, neque facere tuum est."*[70] Whence

[69] Suetonius (70?-140?) *De vita Caesarum* i. 41. The word "sortitus" seems to have been erroneously used in place of "partitus." Thus, the passage should read, "He shared the elections with the people."

[70] "For I would not have you think that I am advising you to enslave the senate and the people and then to set up a tyranny. This is a thing I should never dare to suggest to you, nor would you bring yourself to do it." Dio Cassius *Historiae romanae* . . . lii. 15. (The translation is that of E. Cary, from the Loeb edition, VI, 112f.)

this empire, being neither hawk nor buzzard, made flight accordingly, and having the avarice of the soldiery on this hand to satisfy upon the people, and the senate and the people on the other to be defended from the soldiery, the prince being perpetually tossed seldom died any other death than by one horn of this dilemma, as is noted more at large by Machiavelli.[71] But the pretorian bands, those bestial executioners of their captain's tyranny upon others and of their own upon him, having continued from the time of Augustus, were by Constantine the Great (incensed against them for taking part with his adversary, Maxentius) removed from their strong garrison which they held in Rome, and distributed into divers provinces. The *benefices* of the soldiers that were hitherto held for life and upon duty, were by this prince made hereditary so that the whole foundation whereupon this empire was first built, being now removed, shows plainly that the emperors must long before this have found out some other way of support, and this was by stipendiating the Goths, a people that, deriving their roots from the Northern parts of Germany or out of Sweden, had (through their victories obtained against Domitian) long since spread their branches to so near neighborhood with the Roman territories that they began to overshade them. For the emperors, making use of them in their arms (as the French do at this day of the Swiss), gave them that, under the notion of stipend, which they received as tribute, coming (if there were any default in the payment) so often to distrain for it that in the time of Honorius they sacked Rome and possessed themselves of Italy. And such was the *transition* of *ancient* into *modern prudence,* or that breach which, being followed in every part of the Roman Empire with inundations of Vandals, Huns, Lombards, Franks, Saxons, overwhelmed ancient languages, learning, prudence, manners, cities; changing the names of rivers, countries, seas, mountains, and men; Camillus, Caesar, and Pompey being come to Edmund, Richard, and Geoffrey.

To open the groundwork or balance of these new politi-

[71] *The Prince,* Chap. XIX, 8.

cians, *feudum,* says Calvin the lawyer,[72] is a Gothic word of divers significations, for it is taken either for war or for a "possession of conquered lands distributed by the victor unto such of his captains and soldiers as had merited in his wars, upon condition to acknowledge him to be their perpetual lord and themselves to be his subjects."

Of these there were three kinds or orders. The first, of nobility, distinguished by the titles of dukes, marquesses, earls, and these being gratified with cities, castles, and villages of the conquered Italians, their feuds participated of royal dignity and were called "Regalia," by which they had right to coin money, create magistrates, take toll, customs, confiscations, and the like.

Feuds of the second order were such as with the consent of the king were bestowed by these feudatory princes upon men of inferior quality called their barons, on condition that next unto the king they should defend the dignities and fortunes of their lords in arms.

The lowest order of feuds were such as being conferred by those of the second order upon private men, whether noble or not noble, obliged them in the like duty unto their superiors, these were called "vavasors." *And this is the Gothic balance by which all the kingdoms this day in Christendom were at first erected.* For which cause, if I had time, I should open in this place the Empire of Germany and the kingdoms of France, Spain, and Poland. But so much as has been said being sufficient for the discovery of the principles of *modern prudence in general,* I shall divide the remainder of my discourse, which is more particular, into three parts:

The first, showing the constitution of the late monarchy of
    Oceana;
The second, the dissolution of the same;

[72] This is not John Calvin the theologian, but rather Jean Calvinus, a professor at Heidelberg and author of the *Lexicon juridicum* (Frankfort, 1600); the passage cited by Harrington appears on p. 368 of the 1645 Geneva ed.

And the third, the generation of the present commonwealth.

The constitution of the late monarchy of Oceana is to be
considered in relation to the different nations by whom it
has been successively subdued and governed. The first of
these were the Romans, the second the Teutons [Saxons], the
third the Scandians [Danes], and the fourth the Neustrians
[Normans].

The government of the Romans, who held it as a province,
I shall omit because I am to speak of their provincial government in another place. Only it is to be remembered in this,
that if we have given over running up and down naked and
with dappled hides, learned to write and read, to be instructed
with good arts—for all these we are beholden to the Romans
either immediately or mediately by the Teutons. For that the
Teutons had the arts from no other hand is plain enough by
their language which has yet no word to signify either writing
or reading but what is derived from the Latin. Furthermore,
by the help of these arts so learned we have been capable of
that religion which we have long since received. Wherefore
it seems to me that we ought not to detract from the memory
of the Romans by whose means we are as it were of beasts
become men, and by whose means we might yet of obscure
and ignorant men (if we thought not too well of ourselves)
become a wise and a great people.

The Romans having governed Oceana provincially, the
Teutons were the first that introduced the form of the late
monarchy. To these succeeded the Scandians of whom (because their reign was short, as also because they made little
alteration in the government as to the form) I shall take no
notice. But the Teutons, going to work upon the Gothic balance, divided the whole nation into three sorts of feuds: that
of ealdorman, that of king's thane, and that of middle thane.[73]

[73] At this point Harrington inserts a marginal note reading, "For the
proof of the ensuing discourse out of Records and Antiquities. See
Selden's Titles of Honour, from page 593 to page 837." The reference is
to John Selden, *Titles of Honour*, 2d ed. (London 1631).

When the kingdom was first divided into precincts will be as hard to show as when it began first to be governed, it being impossible that there should be any government without some division. The division that was in use with the Teutons was by counties, and every county had either its ealdorman or high reeve. The title of ealdorman came in time to eorl or earl, and that of high reeve to high sheriff.

Earl of the shire or county denoted the king's thane or tenant by grand sergeantry or knight's service in chief or *in capite*. His possessions were sometimes the whole territory from whence he had his denomination, that is, the whole county, sometimes more than one county, and sometimes less, the remaining part being in the crown. He had also sometimes a third or some other customary part of the profits of certain cities, boroughs, or other places within his earldom. For an example of the possessions of earls in ancient times, Ethelred had unto him and his heirs the whole kingdom of Mercia containing three or four counties, and there were others that had little less.

King's thane was also an honorary title unto which he was qualified that had five hides of land held immediately of the king by service of personal attendance, insomuch that if a churl or country man had thriven unto this proportion, having a church, a kitchen, a bellhouse (that is a hall with a bell in it to call his family to dinner), a borough gate with a seat (that is, a porch) of his own and any distinct office in the king's court—then was he the king's thane. But the proportion of a hide land, otherwise called *caruca* or a ploughland, is difficult to be understood because it was not certain; nevertheless, it is generally conceived to be so much as may be managed with one plough and would yield the maintenance of the same with the appurtenances in all kinds.

The middle thane was feudal but not honorary. He was also called a vavasor and his lands a vavasory, which [he] held of some mesne lord and not immediately of the king.

Possessions and their tenures being of this nature show the balance of the Teuton monarchy, wherein the riches of earls was so vast that to arise from the balance of their dominion unto their power, they were not only called *reguli* or little kings but were such indeed, their jurisdiction being of two sorts, either that which was exercised by them in the court of their counties or in the high court of the kingdom.

In the territory denominating an earl, if it were all his own, the courts held and the profits of that jurisdiction were to his own use and benefit. But if he had but some part of his county, then his jurisdiction and courts (saving perhaps in those possessions that were his own) were held by him to the king's use and benefit; that is, he commonly supplied the office which the sheriffs regularly executed in counties that had no earls and whence they came to be called *vice comites*. The court of the county that had an earl was held by the earl and the bishop of the diocese after the manner of the sheriff's turns unto this day; by which means both the ecclesiastical and temporal laws were given in charge together unto the country. The causes [i.e., cases] of vavasors or vavasories appertained to the cognizance of this court, where wills were proved, judgment and execution given, cases criminal and civil determined.

The king's thanes had like jurisdiction in their thanelands as lords in their manors, where they also kept courts.

Besides these in particular, both the earls and king's thanes, together with the bishops, abbots, and vavasors or middle thanes, had in the High Court or Parliament of the Kingdom a more public jurisdiction consisting, first, of deliberative power for advising upon and assenting to new laws; secondly, of giving counsel in matters of state; and thirdly, of judicature upon suits and complaints. I shall not omit to enlighten the obscurity of these times, in which there is little to be found of a *methodical constitution* of this High Court, by the addition of an argument which I conceive to bear a strong testimony to itself, though taken out of a late writing that conceals the author: [74]

[74] Συλλογολογία, or, *An Historical Discourse of Parliaments* . . . (London, 1656), p. 21.

It is well known (says he) that in every quarter of the realm a great many boroughs do yet send burgesses to the Parliament, which nevertheless be so anciently and so long since decayed and gone to naught that they cannot be shown to have been of any reputation since the Conquest, much less to have obtained any such privilege by the grant of any succeeding king. Wherefore these must have had this right by more ancient usage and before the Conquest, they being unable now to show whence they derived it.

This argument (though there be more) I shall pitch upon as sufficient to prove: first, that the lower sort of the people had right to session in parliament during the time of the Teutons; secondly, that they were qualified unto the same by election in their boroughs and (if knights of the shire, as no doubt they are, be as ancient) in the counties; thirdly, if it be a good argument to say that the Commons during the reign of the Teutons were elected into parliament, because they are so now and no man can show when this custom began, I see not which way it should be an ill one to say that the Commons during the reign of the Teutons constituted also a distinct house, because they do so now, unless any man can show that they did ever sit in the same house with the Lords. Wherefore, to conclude this part, I conceive for these and other reasons to be mentioned hereafter that the parliament of the Teutons consisted of the king, the lords spiritual and temporal, and the Commons of the nation, notwithstanding the style of divers acts of parliament [75] which runs as that of Magna Charta in the king's name only, seeing the same was nevertheless enacted by the king, peers, and commons of the land, as is testified in those words by a subsequent act.

The monarchy of the Teutons had stood in this posture

[75] Harrington in a marginal note here cites 25 Edward III, c. 1, which begins: "Nostre Seignur le Roi, a son parlement tenuz a Westminster . . . par assent de Prelatz, Countz, Barons & autres grantz, & tote la Communalte de son dit roialme. . . ." Liljegren notes the opening words of 25 Edward I, c. 3: "Edward par la grace de dieu, Roy Dengleterre . . . a toutz ceus qui cestes presentes lettres verront ou orront saluz. Sachiez nous al honeur de dieu, & de seinte eglise & au profit de tut nostre Roiaume, aver grante. . . ."

about two hundred and twenty years when Turbo, Duke of Neustria,[76] making his claim to the crown of one of their kings that died childless, followed it with successful arms. And being possessed of the kingdom, used it as conquered, distributing the earldoms, thanelands, bishoprics, and prelacies of the whole realm among his Neustrians. From this time the earl came to be called *comes, consul,* and *dux* (though *consul* and *dux* grew afterward out of use). The king's thanes came to be called barons and their lands baronies. The middle thane holding still of a mean lord, retained the name of vavasor.

The earl or comes continued to have the third part of the pleas of the county paid unto him by the sheriff or vicecomes, now a distinct officer in every county depending upon the king, saving that such earls as had their counties to their own use were now counts palatine and had under the king regal jurisdiction, insomuch that they constituted their own sheriffs, granted pardons, and issued writs in their own names. Nor did king's writ of ordinary justice run in their dominions till a late statute whereby much of this privilege was taken away.[77]

For barons, they came from henceforth to be in different times of three kinds: barons by their estates and tenures, barons by writ, and barons created by *letters patent*. From Turbo the first to Adoxus [78] the seventh king from the conquest, barons had their denomination from their possessions and tenures, and these were either spiritual or temporal. For not only the thanelands, but the possessions of bishops as also of some twenty-six abbots and two priors were now erected into baronies, whence the lords spiritual that had suffrage in the Teuton parliament as spiritual lords came to

[76] Harrington's name for William, Duke of Normandy (1027?-1087); king of England (1066-1087). Probably after Marcus Turbo, who was sent by Trajan to quell a rebellion in Cyrene and did so with singular efficiency.

[77] The statute is 27 Henry VIII, c. 24, "An Acte for recontinuing of certain liberties and franchises heretofore taken from the Crown."

[78] Axodus is King John (1167-1216); from the Greek, "without glory."

have it in the Neustrian parliament as barons and were made subject, which they had not formerly been, unto knight's service in chief. Barony coming henceforth to signify all honorary possessions as well of earls as barons, and baronage to denote all kinds of lords as well spiritual as temporal, having right to sit in parliament, the baronies in this sense were sometimes more and sometimes fewer, but commonly about 200 or 250, containing in them a matter of sixty thousand *feuda militum* or knight's fees, whereof some twenty-eight thousand were in the clergy. It is ill luck that no man can tell what the land of a knight's fee (reckoned in some writs at forty pounds a year and in others at ten) was certainly worth; for by such a help we might have exactly demonstrated the *balance* of this *government*. But, says Cook,[79] it contained twelve plough lands and that was thought to be the most certain account; but this again is extremely uncertain, for one plough out of some land that was fruitful might work more than ten out of some other that was barren. Nevertheless, seeing it appears by Bracton,[80] that of earldoms and baronies, it was wont to be said that the whole kingdom was composed; as also, that these consisting of sixty thousand knight's fees furnished sixty thousand men for the king's service, being the whole militia of this monarchy, it cannot be imagined that the vavasories or freeholds in the people amounted to any considerable proportion. Wherefore the balance and foundation of this government was in the sixty thousand knight's fees and these being possessed by the two hundred and fifty lords, it was a *government* of the *few* or of the *nobility*, wherein the people might also assemble, but could have no more than a mere name. And the clergy holding a third to the whole nation, as is plain by the parliament roll, it is an absurdity (seeing the clergy of France came first through their

---

[79] Sir Edward Coke (1552-1634), Lord Chief Justice of England, *The Institutes of the Laws of England* (London, 1642), II, 596.

[80] Henry Bracton (c. 1210-1268), *The Laws and Customs of England*, II, 34.1; actually Harrington's source was Selden's *Titles of Honour*, II, 5.2, which cites Bracton in a marginal note.

riches to be a state of that kingdom) to acknowledge the people to have been a state of this realm [81] and not allow it unto the clergy, who were so much more weighty in the balance, which is that of all other whence a state or order in a government is denominated. Wherefore this monarchy consisted of the king and of the three estates (or *ordines regni*), the lords spiritual and temporal, and the commons. It consisted of these, I say, as to the balance, though during the reign of some of these kings not as to the administration.

For the ambition of Turbo and some of those that more immediately succeeded him to be absolute princes strove against the nature of their foundation, and, inasmuch as he had divided almost the whole realm among his Neustrians, with some encouragement for a while. But the Neustrians, while they were but foreign plants having no security against the natives but in growing up by their prince's sides, were no sooner well rooted in their vast dominions than they came up, according to the infallible consequence of the balance domestic, and contracting the national interest of the baronage grew as fierce in the vindication of the ancient rights and liberties of the same as if they had been always natives. Whence, the kings being as obstinate on the one side for their absolute power as these on the other for their immunities, grew certain wars which took their denomination from the barons. [82]

This fire about the middle of the reign of Adoxus began to break out. And whereas the predecessors of this king had divers times been forced to summon councils, resembling those of the Teutons, to which the lords only that were barons by dominion and tenure had hitherto repaired, Adoxus seeing the effects of such dominion began first (not to call such as

[81] By "state" Harrington means what is now commonly called an "estate" of the realm. In a marginal note he here cites the Parliament Roll IV Richard II, 13, which refers to "le Clergie que occupie la tierce partie del Roialme. . . ."

[82] The so-called Barons' Wars of the reign of John; the granting of Magna Charta in 1215 was an incident in this continuing struggle.

were barons by writs, for that was according to the practice of ancient times, but) to call such by writs as were otherwise no barons, by which means striving to avoid the consequence of the balance, in coming unwillingly to set the government straight, he was the first that set it awry. For the barons in his reign and his successors', having vindicated their ancient authority, restored the parliament with all the rights and privileges of the same, saving that from thenceforth the kings had found out a way whereby to help themselves against the mighty creatures of their own and such as had no other support but by their favor. By which means this government being indeed the *masterpiece of modern prudence* has been cried up to the skies as the only invention whereby at once to maintain the sovereignty of a prince and the liberty of the people, whereas indeed it has been no other than a wrestling match wherein the nobility as they have been stronger have thrown the king; or the king if he has been stronger has thrown the nobility; or the king where he has had a nobility and could bring them to his party has thrown the people, as in France and Spain; or the people where they have had no nobility or could get them to be of their party have thrown the king, as in Holland and of latter times in Oceana. But they came not to this strength but by such approaches and degrees as remain to be further opened. For whereas the barons by writs (as the sixty-four abbots and thirty-six priors that were so called) were but *pro tempore,* Dicotome,[83] being the twelfth king from the conquest, began to make barons by *letters patent* with the addition of honorary pensions for the maintenance of their dignities to them and their heirs, so that they were hands in the king's purse and had no shoulders for his throne. Of these, when the house of peers came once to be full, as will be seen hereafter, there was nothing more empty. But for the present, the throne having other supports, they did not hurt that so much as they did the king. For the

---

[83] Dicotome is Richard II (1367-1400), king from 1377 until his deposition in 1399. The name probably comes from the Greek meaning "cutting in two."

old barons, taking Dicotome's prodigality to such creatures so ill that they deposed him, got the trick of it, and never gave over setting up and pulling down of their kings according to their various interests, and that faction of the White and Red into which they had been thenceforth divided, till Panurgus [84] the eighteenth, king from the conquest was more by their favor than his right advanced to the crown. This king through his natural subtility, reflecting at once upon the greatness of their power and the inconstancy of their favor, began to find another flaw in this kind of government, which is also noted by Machiavelli, namely, that a throne supported by a nobility is not so hard to be ascended as kept warm.[85] Wherefore his secret jealousy lest the dissension of the nobility, as it brought him in, might throw him out, traveled in ways undiscovered by them unto ends as little foreseen by himself. While to establish his own safety he, by mixing water with their wine, first began to open those sluices that have since overwhelmed not the king only, but the throne. For whereas a nobility strikes not at the throne without which they cannot subsist, but at some king that they do not like, popular power strikes through the king at the throne, as that which is incompatible with it. Now that Panurgus in abating the power of the nobility was the cause whence it came to fall into the hands of the people appears by those several statutes that were made in his reign, as that for population, those against retainers, and that for alienations.

By the Statute of Population,[86] all houses of husbandry that were used with twenty acres of ground and upward were to be maintained and kept up for ever with a competent proportion of land laid to them, and in no wise, as appears by a subsequent statute, to be severed. By which means the houses being kept up, did of necessity enforce dwellers, and the proportion of land to be tilled being kept up, did of necessity

[84] Panurgus is Henry VII (1457-1509); king (1485-1509).

[85] *The Prince*, Chap. IV.

[86] The Statute of Population is 4 Henry VII, c. 19, "An Acte against pulling down of towns."

enforce the dweller not to be a beggar or cottager, but a man of some substance that might keep hinds and servants and set the plough on going. This did mightily concern (says the historian of that prince) [87] the might and manhood of the kingdom, and in effect amortize a great part of the lands to the hold and possession of the yeomanry or middle people, who living not in a servile or indigent fashion were much unlinked from dependence upon their lords, and living in a free and plentiful manner became a more excellent infantry, but such a one upon which the lords had so little power that from henceforth they may be computed to have been disarmed.

And as they lost their infantry after this manner, so their cavalry and commanders were cut off by the Statute of Retainers. [88] For whereas it was the custom of the nobility to have younger brothers of good houses, "metalled fellows," and such as were knowing in the feats of arms about them, they who were longer followed with so dangerous a train, escaped not such punishments as made them take up.

Henceforth the country-lives and great tables of the nobility, which no longer nourished veins that would bleed for them, were fruitless and loathsome till they changed the air and of princes became courtiers, where their revenues, never to have been exhausted by beef and mutton, were found narrow, whence followed wracking of rents and, at length, sale of lands, the riddance through the Statute of Alienations [89] being rendered far more quick and facile than formerly it had been through the new invention of *entails*.

To this it happened that Coraunus, [90] the successor of that king, dissolving the abbeys brought with the declining estate

[87] Francis Bacon, *Historia regni regis Henrici VII* (Leyden, 1642), pp. 131f.

[88] The Statute of Retainers is 19 Henry VII, c. 14, *"De retentionibus illicitis."*

[89] The Statute of Alienations is 4 Henry VII, c. 4, "An Acte for the passing and transmutation of lands without fine."

[90] Coraunus is Henry VIII (1491-1547); king (1509-1547). The name alludes to his numerous wives.

of the nobility so vast a prey to the industry of the people that the balance of the commonwealth was too apparently in the popular party to be unseen by the wise counsel of Queen Parthenia [91] who, converting her reign through the perpetual love tricks that passed between her and her people into a kind of romance, wholly neglected the nobility. And by these degrees came the House of Commons to raise that head which since has been so high and formidable to their princes that they have looked pale upon those assemblies. Nor was there anything now wanting to the destruction of the throne but that the people, not apt to see their own strength, should be put to feel it. When a prince,[92] as stiff in disputes as the nerve of monarchy was grown slack, received that unhappy encouragement from his clergy which became his utter ruin, while trusting more to their logic than [to] the rough philosophy of his parliament, it came to an irreparable breach, for the house of Peers which alone had stood in this gap, now sinking down between the king and the commons, showed that Crassus was dead and Isthmus broken. But a monarchy divested of her nobility has no refuge under heaven but an army. *Wherefore the dissolution of this government caused the war, not the war the dissolution of this government.*

Of the king's success with his arms, it is not necessary to give any further account than that they proved as ineffectual as his nobility. But without a nobility or an army (as has been shown) there can be no monarchy. Wherefore what is there in nature that can arise out of these ashes but a popular government or a new monarchy to be erected by the victorious army?

To erect a monarchy be it never so new, unless like Hobbes, you hang it (as the country fellow speaks) by geometry (for what else is it to say that every other man must give up his

[91] Parthenia is Elizabeth (1533-1603); queen (1558-1603). The name means "virgin."

[92] This probably refers to Charles I (1600-1649), king (1625-1649), although the description fits his father, James I (1566-1625), king of England (1603-1625), equally well.

will unto the will of this one man without any other foundation?), it must stand upon old principles, that is, upon nobility or an army planted upon a due balance of dominion. *Aut
viam inveniam aut faciam*,[93] was an adage of Caesar's, and
there is no standing for a monarchy unless she find this balance or make it. If she find it, her work's done unto her hand;
for where there is inequality of estates, there must be inequality of power, and where there is inequality of power, there
can be no commonwealth. To make it, her sword must extirpate out of dominion all other roots of power and plant her
army upon that ground; an army may be planted nationally
or provincially. To plant it nationally, it must be in one of
the four ways mentioned, that is, either monarchically in part
as the Roman *beneficiarii,* or monarchically in the whole as
the Turkish timariot, aristocratically, that is, by earls and
barons as the Neustrians were planted by Turbo, or democratically, that is, by equal lots, as the Israelite army in the
land of Canaan by Joshua. In every one of these ways there
must not only be confiscations, but confiscations to such a
proportion as may answer to the work intended.

Confiscation of a people that never fought against you but
whose arms you have borne and in which you have been victorious, and this upon premeditation and in cool blood, I
should have thought to be against any example in human
nature but for those alleged by Machiavelli of Agathocles and
Oliveretto da Fermo.[94] The former whereof being captain
general of the Syracusans, upon a day assembled the senate
and the people as if he had something to communicate with
them, when at a sign given, he cut the senators in pieces to
a man and all the richest of the people, by which means he
came to be king. The proceedings of Oliveretto in making
himself prince of Fermo was somewhat different in circumstances, but of the same nature. Nevertheless, Catiline, who
had a spirit equal to any of these in his intended mischief,

93 "Either find a way or make one."
94 *The Prince,* Chap. VIII ("Of those who have attained the position of
prince by villainy.").

could never bring the like to pass in Rome. The head of a small commonwealth, such a one as was that of Syracuse or Fermo, is easily brought unto the block, but that a populous nation such as Rome had not such a one was the grief of Nero. If Sylla or Caesar attained to be princes, it was by civil war and such civil war as yielded rich spoils, there being a vast nobility to be confiscated, which also was the case in Oceana when it yielded earth by earldoms and baronies to the Neustrian for the plantation of his new potentates. Where a conqueror finds the riches of a land in the hands of the few, the forfeitures are easy and amount to vast advantage. But where the people have equal shares, the confiscation of many comes to little and is not only dangerous, but fruitless.

The Romans in one of their defeats of the Volsci found among the captives certain Tusculans, who upon examination confessed that the arms they bore were by command of their state.[95] Whereupon information being given to the senate by the general Camillus, he was forthwith commanded to march against Tusculum. Which doing accordingly, he found the Tusculan fields full of husbandmen that stirred not otherwise from the plough than to furnish his army with all kind of accommodations and victuals. Drawing near to the city, he saw the gates wide open, the magistrates coming out in their gowns to salute and bid him welcome; entering, the shops were all at work and open, the streets sounded with the noise of schoolboys at their books, there was no face of war. Whereupon Camillus, causing the senate to assemble, told them that though the art was understood, yet had they at length found out the true arms whereby the Romans were most undoubtedly to be conquered, for which cause he would not anticipate the senate, unto which he desired them forthwith to send, which they did accordingly. And their dictator with the rest of their ambassadors being found by the Roman senators as they went into the house standing sadly at the door, were sent for in as friends, and not as enemies. Where the dictator having said, "If we have offended, the fault was not so great

95 The story told in this paragraph is found in Livy vi. 25ff.

as is our penitence and your virtue," the senate gave them peace forthwith, and soon after made the Tusculans citizens of Rome.

But putting the case of which the world is not able to show an example, that the forfeiture of a populous nation, not conquered, but friends and in cool blood, might be taken, your army must be planted in one of the ways mentioned. To plant it in the way of absolute monarchy, that is upon feuds for life, such as the timars, a country as large and fruitful as that of Greece, would afford you but sixteen thousand timariots, for that is the most the Turk (being the best husband that ever was of this kind) makes of it at this day. And if Oceana which is less in fruitfulness by one half, and in extent by three parts, should have no greater a force, whoever breaks her in one battle may be sure she shall never rise; for such (as was noted by Machiavelli) [96] is the nature of the Turkish monarchy—if you break her in two battles, you have destroyed her whole militia, and the rest being all slaves, you hold her without any further resistance. Wherefore the erection of an absolute monarchy in Oceana, or in any other country that is no larger, without making it a certain prey unto the first invader is altogether impossible.

To plant by halves, as the Roman Emperors did their beneficiaries or military colonies, it must be either for life, and this an army of Oceaners in their own country (especially having states of inheritance) will never bear because such an army so planted is as well confiscated as the people, nor had the Mamelukes been contented with such usage in Egypt, but that they were foreigners and, daring not to mix with the natives, it was of absolute necessity to their being.

Or planting them upon inheritance, whether aristocratically as the Neustrians, or democratically as the Israelites, they grow up by certain consequence into the *national interest,* and this if they be planted popularly comes to a commonwealth, if by way of nobility to a mixed monarchy, which of all other will be found to be the only kind of monarchy

[96] *The Prince,* Chap. IV.

whereof this nation or any other that is of no greater extent has been or can be capable. For if the Israelites (though their democratic balance being fixed by their Agrarian stood firm) be yet found to have elected kings, it was because their territory lying open they were perpetually invaded, and being perpetually invaded turned themselves to anything which through the want of experience they thought might be a remedy. Whence their mistake in election of their kings (under whom they gained nothing, but to the contrary lost all they had acquired by their commonwealth, both estates and liberties) is not only apparent, but without parallel. And if there have been (as was shown) a kingdom of the Goths in Spain and of the Vandals in Asia consisting of a single person and a parliament (taking parliament to be a council of the people only without a nobility), it is expressly said of those councils that they deposed their kings as often as they pleased. Nor can there be other consequence of such a government, seeing where there is a council of the people they do never receive laws, but give them; and a council giving laws to a single person, he has no means in the world whereby to be any more than a subordinate magistrate, but force. In which case, he is not a single person and a parliament, but a single person and an army, which army again must be planted as has been shown or can be of no long continuance.

It is true that the provincial balance being in nature quite contrary to the national, you are no ways to plant a provincial army upon dominion. But then you must have a native territory in strength, situation, or government able to overbalance the foreign or you can never hold it. That an army should in any other case be long supported by a mere tax, is a mere fancy as void of all reason and experience as if a man should think to maintain such a one by robbing of orchards. For a mere tax is but pulling of plum trees, the roots whereof are in other men's grounds, who suffering perpetual violence come to hate the author of it. And it is a maxim that *no prince that is hated by his people can be safe*.[97] Arms planted upon

[97] *Ibid.*, Chap. **XI**.

dominion extirpate enemies and make friends, but maintained by a mere tax have enemies that have roots and friends that have none.

To conclude, Oceana, or any other nation of no greater extent, must have a competent nobility or is altogether incapable of monarchy. *For where there is equality of estates, there must be equality of power, and where there is equality of power, there can be no monarchy.*

To come then to the generation of the commonwealth: it has been shown how through the ways and means used by Panurgus to abase the nobility, and so to mend that flaw which we have asserted to be incurable in this kind of constitution, he suffered the balance to fall into the power of the people, and so broke the government. But the balance being in the people, the commonwealth (though they do not see it) is already in the nature of them (*Cornua nota prius Vitulo, quam frontibus extant*).[98] There wants nothing else but time (which is slow and dangerous) or art (which would be more quick and secure) for the bringing those native arms (wherewithal they are found already) to resist, they know not how, everything that opposes them unto such maturity as may fix them upon their own strength and bottom.

But whereas this art is prudence, and that part of prudence which regards the present work is nothing else but the skill of raising such superstructures of government as are natural to the known foundations: they never mind the foundation but through certain animosities (wherewith by striving one against another they are infected), or through freaks by which not regarding the course of things, nor how they conduce unto their purpose, they are given to building in the air, come to be divided and subdivided into endless parties and factions both civil and ecclesiastical; which briefly to open, I shall first speak of the people in general and then of their divisions.

[98] "Before the budding horns stand out on the calf's forehead [these are what he uses in anger to butt with. . . .]" Lucretius *De rerum natura* v. 1032.

A people (says Machiavelli) [99] that is corrupt is not capable of a commonwealth. But in showing what a corrupt people is, he has either involved himself or me, nor can I otherwise come out of the labyrinth than by saying that, the balance altering, a people as to the foregoing government must of necessity be corrupt. But corruption in this sense signifies no more than that the *corruption of one government* (as in natural bodies) *is the generation of another*. Wherefore, if the balance alter from monarchy, the corruption of the people in this case is that which makes them capable of a commonwealth. But whereas I am not ignorant that the corruption which he means is in manners, this also is from the balance. For the balance swaying from monarchical into popular abates the luxury of the nobility and, enriching the people, brings the government from a more private to a more public interest, which coming nearer, as has been shown, to justice and right reason, the people upon a like alteration is so far from such corruption of manners as should render them incapable of a commonwealth, that of necessity they must thereby contract such reformation of manners as will bear no other kind of government. On the other side, where the balance changes from popular to oligarchical or monarchical, the public interest with the reason and justice included in the same becomes more private, luxury is introduced in the place of temperance, and servitude in that of freedom. Which causes such a corruption of manners both in the nobility and the people as, by the example of Rome in the time of the triumvirate, is more at large discovered by the author to have been altogether incapable of a commonwealth.

But the balance of Oceana changing quite contrary to that of Rome, the manners of the people were not thereby corrupted, but on the contrary fitted for a commonwealth. For differences of opinion in a people (not rightly informed of their balance) or division into parties while there is not any common ligament of power sufficient to reconcile or hold them, is no sufficient proof of corruption in a people. Never-

[99] *Discourses*, I, 17.

theless, seeing this must needs be matter of scandal and danger, it will not be amiss in showing what were the parties to show what were their errors.

The parties into which this nation was divided were temporal or spiritual; and the temporal parties were especially two, the one the royalists, the other commonwealths-men. Each of which asserted their different causes, either out of prudence or ignorance, out of interest or conscience.

For prudence, either that of the ancients is inferior to the modern (which we have hitherto been setting face to face, that anyone may judge) or that of the royalists must be inferior to that of the commonwealths-man; and for interest, taking the commonwealths-man to have really intended the public (for otherwise he is a hypocrite and the worst of men), that of the royalist must of necessity have been more private; wherefore, the whole dispute will come upon matter of conscience, and this, whether it be urged by the right of kings, the obligation of former laws, or of the Oath of Allegiance, is absolved by the balance.

For if the right of kings were as immediately derived from the breath of God as the life of man, yet this excludes not death and dissolution. But that the dissolution of the late monarchy was as natural as the death of a man has been already shown. Wherefore it remains with the royalists to discover by what reason or experience it is possible for a monarchy to stand upon a popular balance, or the balance being popular, as well the Oath of Allegiance as all other monarchical laws, imply an impossibility and are therefore void.

To the commonwealths-man I have no more to say but that if he exclude any party, he is not truly such nor shall ever found a commonwealth upon the natural principle of the same, which is justice. And the royalist for having opposed a commonwealth in Oceana (where the laws were so ambiguous that they might be eternally disputed and never reconciled) can neither be justly for that cause excluded from his full and equal share in the government. Nor prudently, for this [reason], that a commonwealth consisting of a party will be in perpetual labor of her own destruction. Whence it was that the Romans, having conquered the Albans, incorporated them with equal right into the commonwealth. And if the royalists be flesh of your flesh and nearer of blood than were the Albans to the Romans, you are also Christians; nevertheless, there is no reason that a commonwealth should any more favor a party remaining in fixed opposition against her than Brutus did his sons. But if she fix them upon that opposition, it is her fault not theirs, and this is done by excluding them. Men that have equal possessions and the same security of their estates and of their liberties that you have, have the same cause with you to defend. But if you will be trampling, they fight for liberty, though for monarchy, and you for tyranny, though under the name of a commonwealth; the nature of orders in a commonwealth rightly instituted being void of all jealousy because, let the parties which she embraces be what they will, her orders are such as they neither would resist if they could nor could if they would, as has in part been already shown and will appear more at large by the ensuing Model.

The parties that are spiritual are of more kinds than I need mention, some for a national religion and others for liberty of conscience, with such animosity on both sides as if these two did not consist, of which I have already sufficiently spoken to show that the one cannot well consist without the other. But they of all the rest are the most dangerous who, holding that the saints must govern, go about to reduce the commonwealth to a party, as well for the reasons already shown as that their pretenses are against Scripture, where the saints are commanded to submit to the higher powers and be subject to the ordinance of man. [100] And that men pretending under the notion of saints or religion to civil power have hitherto never

100 See Rom. 13:1ff.: "Let every person be subject to the governing authorities. For there is no authority except from God, and those that exist have been ordained by God. . . ."

failed to dishonor that profession, the world is full of examples, whereof I shall confine myself at the present to two, the
one of old, the other of new Rome.

In old Rome the patricians or nobility, pretending to be
the godly party, were questioned by the people for engrossing
all the magistracies of that commonwealth, and had nothing
to say why they did so but *(Quod nemo plebeius auspicia
haberet)* that magistracy required a kind of holiness which
was not in the people. *Plebs ad id maxima indignatione
exarsit, quod auspicari tanquam invisi Diis immortalibus
negarentur posse,*[101] at which the people were filled with such
indignation as had come to cutting of throats if the nobility
had not forthwith laid by the insolence of that plea; which
nevertheless when they had done, the people for a long time
after continued to elect none other than patrician magistrates.

The example of new Rome in the rise and practice of the
hierarchy, too well known to require any further illustration,
is far more immodest.[102]

This has been the course of nature; and when it has pleased
or shall please God to introduce anything that is above the
course of nature he will, as he has always done, confirm it by
miracle; for so in his prophecy of the reign of Christ upon
earth he expressly promises,[103] seeing that "the souls of them
that were beheaded for Jesus, shall be seen to live and reign
with him, which will be an object of sense," the rather because
the rest of the dead are not to live again until the thousand
years be finished. And it is not lawful for men to persuade us
that a thing is, though there be no such object of our sense,
which God has told us shall not be until it be an object of our
sense.

The saintship of a people as to government consists in the

---

[101] Both quotations are from Livy iv. 6. In translation they are: (a)
"that no plebeian could have the auspices," and (b) "the plebeians were
indignant with this above all because, as if hateful to the gods, they were
denied the auspices."

[102] The "new Rome" is, of course, the papacy.

[103] Rev. 20:4f.

election of magistrates fearing God and hating covetousness and not in their confining themselves or being confined to men of this or that party or profession. It consists in making the most prudent and religious choice that they can, but not in trusting to men, but, next [to] God, in their orders. "Give us good men and they will make us good laws" is the maxim of a demagogue and (through the alteration which is commonly perceivable in men, when they have power to work their own wills) exceedingly fallible. But "give us good orders, and they will make us good men" is the maxim of a legislator, and the most infallible in the politics.[104]

But these divisions (however there be some good men that look sadly on them) are trivial things. First (as to the civil concernment), because the government whereof this nation is capable (the errors of the people are from their governors) once seen takes in all interests. And secondly (as to the spiritual), because as pretense of religion has always been turbulent in broken governments, so where the government has been sound and steady religion has never showed herself with any other face than that of her natural sweetness and tranquility, nor is there any reason why she should. Wherefore the errors of the people are occasioned by their governors. If they be doubtful of the way or wander from it, it is because their guides misled them and the guides of the people are never so well qualified for leading by any virtue of their own as by that of the government.

The government of Oceana (as it stood at the time whereof we discourse, consisting of one single council of the people to the exclusion of the king and of the lords) was called a parliament. How be it the parliaments of the Teutons and of the Neustrians consisted, as has been shown, of the king, lords, and commons, wherefore this under an old name was

104 "Give us good men . . ." is reminiscent of Grotius' statement, "Good governors bring in good customs," *Politick Maxims* (1654), but it is not likely that Harrington had any particular source in mind. "Give us good orders . . ." is reminiscent of the passage from Machiavelli's *Discourses*, I, 3, which reads in part, "the law makes men good."

a new thing: a parliament consisting of a single assembly elected by the people and invested with the whole power of the government without any covenants, conditions, or orders whatsoever. So new a thing that neither ancient nor modern prudence can show any avowed example of the like. And there is scarce anything that seems to me so strange as that (whereas there was nothing more familiar with these counselors than to bring the Scripture to the house) there should be not a man of them that so much as offered to bring the house unto the Scripture, wherein, as has been shown, is contained that original whereof all the rest of the commonwealths seem to be copies. Certainly if Hobbes (who is surer of nothing than that a popular commonwealth consists but of one council) transcribed his doctrine out of this assembly, for him to except against Aristotle and Cicero for writing out of their own commonwealths was not so fair play. Or if the parliament transcribed out of him, it had been an honor better due unto Moses. But where one of them should have an example, but from the other, I cannot imagine, there being nothing of this kind that I can find in [history] but the oligarchy of Athens, the Thirty Tyrants of the same, and the Roman decemvirs.

For the oligarchy, Thucydides [105] tells us that it was a senate or council of four hundred, pretending to a balancing council of the people consisting of five thousand but not producing them, wherein you have the definition of an oligarchy, which is a single council both debating and resolving, dividing and choosing. And what that must come to was shown by the example of the "girls" and is apparent throughout all experience. Wherefore the thirty set up by the Spartans (when they had conquered Athens) are called tyrants by all authors, Hobbes only excepted, who will have them against all the world to have been an aristocracy, but for what reason I cannot imagine, these also as void of any balance having been void of that which is essential to every commonwealth whether aristocratic or popular; except he be pleased with

[105] *History of the Peloponnesian Wars* vii. 67.2f.

them in that by the testimony of Xenophon [106] they killed more men in eight months than the Spartans had done in ten years, oppressing the people (to use Sir Walter Raleigh's words) [107] with all base and intolerable slavery.

The usurped government of the decemvirs in Rome was of the same kind. Wherefore in the fear of God let Christian legislators (setting the pattern given on the Mount on the one side and these execrable examples on the other) know the right hand from the left and so much the rather because those things which do not conduce to the good of the governed are fallacious if they appear to be good for the governors. God in chastising a people is accustomed to burn His rod. The empire of these oligarchies was not so violent as short, nor did they fall upon the people but in their own immediate ruin. A council without a balance is not a commonwealth but an oligarchy, and every oligarchy except she be put to the defense of her wickedness or power against some outward danger is factious. Wherefore the errors of the people being from their governors (which maxim in the politics bearing a sufficient testimony unto itself is also proved by Machiavelli), if the people of Oceana have been factious the cause is apparent; but what remedy?

In answer to this question, I come now to the army of which the most victorious captain and incomparable patriot Olphaus Megaletor was now general.[108] Who, being a much greater master of that art whereof I have made a rough draft in these Preliminaries, had so sad reflections upon the ways and proceedings of the Parliament as cast him upon books and all other means of diversion, among which he happened upon this place of Machiavelli: "Thrice happy is that people which chances to have a man able to give them such a government at once, as without alteration may secure them of their liberties, seeing it is certain that Lacedaemon in observing the laws of Lycurgus continued about eight hundred

[106] *History of Greece* ii. 4.21.
[107] *History of the World*, III, 8.12.
[108] Olphaus Megaletor is Oliver Cromwell. See note p. 74.

years without any dangerous tumult or corruption." [109] My Lord General (as it is said of Themistocles, that he could not sleep for the glory obtained by Miltiades at the battle of Marathon) took so new and deep impression at these words of the much greater glory of Lycurgus, that being on this side assaulted with the emulation of his illustrious object, on the other with the misery of the nation, which seemed (as it were ruined by his victory) to cast herself at his feet, he was almost wholly deprived of his natural rest until the debate he had within himself came to a firm resolution that the greatest advantages of a commonwealth are, first, that the legislator should be one man, and secondly, that the government should be made altogether or at once. For the first it is certain, says Machiavelli,[110] that a commonwealth is seldom or never well turned or constituted except it have been the work of one man. For which cause a wise legislator and one whose mind is firmly set not upon private but the public interest, not upon his posterity but upon his country, may justly endeavor to get the sovereign power into his own hands. Nor shall any man that is master of reason blame such extraordinary means as in that case shall be necessary, the end proving no other than the constitution of a well-ordered commonwealth. The reason of this is demonstrable: for the ordinary means not failing, the commonwealth has no need of a legislator, but the ordinary means failing, there is no recourse to be had but to such as are extraordinary. And, whereas a book or a building has not been known to attain to perfection if it have not had a sole author or architect, a commonwealth, as to the fabric of it, is of the like nature. And thus it may be made at once, in which there be great advantages. For a commonwealth made at once takes her security at the same time she lends her money, trusts not herself to the faith of men, but launches immediately forth into the *empire of laws,* and being set straight, brings the manners of her citizens unto her rule. Whence followed that uprightness which was in Sparta. But

[109] *Discourses,* I, 2.
[110] *Ibid.,* I, 9.

manners that are rooted in men bow the tenderness of a commonwealth coming up by twigs unto their bent; whence followed the obliquity that was in Rome and those perpetual repairs by the consuls' axes and tribunes' hammers, which could never finish that commonwealth but in destruction.

My Lord General being clear in these points and the necessity of some other course than would be thought upon by the Parliament, appointed a rendezvous of the army, where he spoke his sense agreeable to these Preliminaries with such success to the soldiery that the Parliament was soon after deposed, and himself (in the great Hall of the Pantheon or Palace of Justice, situated in Emporium, the capital city) created, by the universal suffrage of the army, Lord Archon, or sole legislator of Oceana; upon which theater you have, to conclude this piece, a person introduced whose fame shall never draw his curtain.[111]

The Lord Archon being created, fifty select persons to assist him (by laboring in the mines of ancient prudence and bringing her hidden treasures unto new light) were added, with the style also of Legislators and sat as a Council whereof he was the sole Director and President.

THE COUNCIL OF LEGISLATORS

Of this piece, being the greater half of the whole work, I shall be able at this time to give no further account than very briefly to show at what it aims.

My Lord Archon in opening the Council of Legislators made it appear how unsafe a thing it is to follow fancy in the fabric of a commonwealth, and how necessary that the archives of ancient prudence should be ransacked before any counselor should presume to offer any other matter in order to the work at hand, or towards the consideration to be had by the Council upon a Model of Government. Wherefore he caused an urn

[111] Pantheon is Westminster Hall; Emporium is London.

to be brought, and every one of the counselors to draw a lot; by the lots as they were drawn:

The Commonwealth of	fell to
Israel,	Phosphorus de Auge
Athens,	Navarchus de Paralo
Sparta,	Laco de Scytale
Carthage,	Mago de Syrtibus
the Achaeans, Aetolians, and Lycians,	Aratus de Isthmo
the Swiss,	Alpester de Fulmine
Holland and the United Provinces,	Glaucus de Ulna
Rome,	Dolabella de Enyo
Venice,	Lynceus de Stella.[112]

These containing in them all those excellencies whereof a commonwealth is capable, so that to have added more had been to no purpose, upon time given to the counselors by their own studies and those of their friends to prepare themselves, [they] were opened in the order, and by the persons mentioned, at the Council of Legislators; and afterwards by order of the same were repeated at the Council of Prytans unto the people (for in drawing of the lots there were a dozen of them inscribed with the letter P, which the counselors that drew became Prytans).

The Prytans were a committee or council sitting in the great Hall of Pantheon, to whom it was lawful for any man to offer anything in order to the fabric of the commonwealth. For which cause, that they might not be oppressed by the throng, there was a rail about the table where they sat, and on each side of the same a pulpit; that on the right hand for any man that would propose anything, and that on the left for any other that would oppose him. And all parties (being

---

[112] For a discussion of the derivations of these fictitious names (none of which apparently was intended to refer to a real person), see Liljegren's edition of *Oceana,* p. 287.

indemnified by proclamation of the Archon) were invited to dispute their own interests, or propose whatever they thought fit (in order to the future government) to the Council of the Prytans, who (having a guard of a matter of two or three hundred men, lest the heat of the dispute might break the peace) had the right of moderators, and were to report from time to time such propositions or occurrences as they thought fit to the Council of Legislators sitting more privately in the palace called Alma.[113]

This was that which made the people (who were neither safely to be admitted unto, nor conveniently to be excluded from, the framing of their commonwealth) verily believe when it came forth that it was no other than that whereof they themselves had been the makers.

Moreover, this Council sat divers months after the publishing and during the promulgation of the Model unto the people, by which means there is scarce anything was said or written for or against the said Model, but you shall have it with the next impression of this work by way of oration addressed unto and moderated by the Prytans.[114]

By this means the Council of Legislators had their necessary solitude and due aim in their greater work, as being acquainted from time to time with the pulse of the people, and yet without any manner of interruption or disturbance.

Wherefore every commonwealth in her place having been opened by her due method, that is, *first,* by the people, *secondly,* by the senate, and *thirdly,* by the magistracy, the Council upon mature debate took such results or orders out of each one, and out of each part of each one of them, as upon opening the same they thought fit. Which, being put from time to time in writing by the clerk or secretary, there re-

[113] The "palace called Alma" is St. James's Palace.

[114] The Prytans, in Athens, were the executive committee of the senate of five hundred. Harrington's reference to "the next impression of this work" is obscure. Perhaps it indicates that he intended in subsequent editions of the *Oceana* to include refutations of arguments which had been brought against his proposals. If this were his intention, he never did so, but his later works are frequently concerned with Harrington's critics.

mained no more in the conclusion than putting the Orders so taken together to view and examine them with a diligent eye, to the end that it might be clearly discovered whether they did interfere, or could any wise come to interfere or jostle one the other. For as such orders jostling, or coming to jostle, one another are the certain dissolution of the commonwealth, so taken upon the proof of like experience, and neither jostling nor showing which way they can possibly come to jostle one another, [they] make a perfect and (for aught that in human prudence can be foreseen) an *immortal commonwealth*.

And such was the art whereby my Lord Archon (taking counsel of the commonwealth of Israel as of Moses, and of the rest of the commonwealths, as of Jethro) [115] framed the Model of the Commonwealth of Oceana.

II

THE AGRARIAN LAW

These selections from *The Commonwealth of Oceana* contain all the material from the third part, "The Model of the Commonwealth of Oceana," pertaining to the so-called Agrarian Law. Included here, after a brief introduction, are the texts of the Law and of two speeches which purport to have been delivered in the Council of Legislators of Oceana. The first speech raises several objections to the Law, and the second, delivered by Harrington's spokesman Olphaus Megaletor, answers each of these. This passage is significant both as an illustration of the form of the third part of the *Oceana* and as a defense by Harrington of one of his most original proposals. The parts reprinted here are found on pages 86-114 of the first edition of *Oceana;* pages 85-99 of Liljegren's edition.

The institution of the Commonwealth was such as needed those props and scaffolds which may have troubled the reader,

115 For Moses and Jethro, see Exod. 18:13-27.

but I shall here take them away and come to the Constitution which stands by itself and yields a clearer prospect.

The motions, by what has been already shown, are spherical, and spherical motions have their proper center, for which cause (ere I proceed further) it will be necessary for the better understanding of the whole that I discover the center whereupon the motions of this Commonwealth are formed.

The center or basis of every government is no other than the fundamental laws of the same.

Fundamental laws are such as state what it is that a man may call his own, that is to say, property, and what the means be whereby a man may enjoy his own, that is to say, protection; the first is also called dominion, and the second, empire or sovereign power, whereof this (as has been shown) is the natural product of the former, for such as is the balance of the dominion in a nation, such is the nature of her empire.

Wherefore the fundamental laws of Oceana, or the center of this Commonwealth, are the Agrarian and the ballot. The Agrarian by the balance of dominion preserving equality in the root, and the ballot by an equal rotation conveying it into the branch or exercise of sovereign power—as to begin with, the former appears by:

The Thirteenth Order, constituting the Agrarian Laws of Oceana, Marpesia [Scotland], and Panopea [Ireland], whereby it is ordained, first, for all such lands as are lying and being within the proper territories of Oceana, that every man who is at present possessed or shall hereafter be possessed of an estate in land exceeding the revenue of two thousands pounds a year, and having more than one son, shall leave his lands either equally divided among them, in case the lands amount unto above two thousand pounds a year unto each, or so near equally, in case they come under, that the greater part or portion of the same remaining unto the eldest exceed not the value of two thousand pounds revenue. And no man not in present possession of lands above the value of two thousand pounds by the year shall receive, enjoy (except by lawful inheritance), acquire, or purchase unto himself lands within the said territories amounting, with those already in his possession, above the said revenue. And if a man have a daughter or daughters, except she be an heir or they be heirs, he shall not leave or give to any one of them, in marriage or otherwise, for her portion above the value of one thousand five hundred pounds in lands, goods, and monies; nor shall any friend, kinsman, or kinswoman add to her or their portion or portions that are so provided for, to make any one of them greater; nor shall any man demand, or have more in marriage, with any woman. Nevertheless, an heir shall enjoy her lawful inheritance, and a widow whatsoever the bounty or affection of her husband shall bequeath unto her, to be divided in the first generation wherein it is divisible according as has been shown.

Secondly, for lands lying and being within the territories of Marpesia, the Agrarian shall hold in all parts as it is established in Oceana, save only in the standard or proportion of estates in land, which shall be set for Marpesia at five hundred pounds.

And thirdly, for Panopea, the Agrarian shall hold in all parts as in Oceana. And whosoever possessing above the proportion allowed by these laws shall be lawfully convicted of the same, shall forfeit the overplus unto the use of the state.

Agrarian laws of all others have ever been the greatest bugbears and so in the institution were these, at which time it was ridiculous to see how strange a fear appeared in everybody of that which, being good for all, could hurt nobody. But instead of the proof of this order, I shall, out of those many debates that happened ere it could be passed, insert two speeches that were made at the Council of Legislators, the first by the Right Honorable Philautus de Garbo,[1] a young

---

[1] From the Greek word meaning "selfish" and the Italian word meaning "politeness."

man being heir apparent to a very noble family and one of the Counselors, who expressed himself as follows:

"May it please your Highness, My Lord Archon of Oceana: If I did not (to my capacity) know from how profound a counselor I dissent, it would certainly be no hard task to make it as light as the day, first, that an Agrarian is altogether unnecessary; secondly, that it is dangerous to a commonwealth; thirdly, that it is insufficient to keep out monarchy; fourthly, that it destroys families; fifthly, that it destroys industry; and last of all, that, though it were indeed of any good use, it will be a matter of such difficulty to introduce in this nation and so to settle that it may be lasting, as is altogether invincible.

"1. First, that an Agrarian is unnecessary to a commonwealth, what clearer testimony can there be than that the commonwealths which are our contemporaries (Venice, whereunto your Highness gives the upper hand of all antiquity, being one) have no such thing? And there can be no reason why they have it not, seeing it is in the sovereign power at any time to establish such an order, but that they need it not; wherefore no wonder if Aristotle, who pretends to be a good commonwealths-man, have long since derided Phaleas (to whom it was attributed by the Greeks) for his invention.[2]

"2. Secondly, that an Agrarian is dangerous to a commonwealth is affirmed upon no slight authority, seeing Machiavelli is positive that it was the dissension which happened about the Agrarian that caused the destruction of Rome,[3] nor do I think that it did much better in Sparta, as I shall show anon.

"3. Thirdly, that it is insufficient to keep out monarchy cannot without impiety be denied, the Holy Scriptures bearing witness that the commonwealth of Israel, notwithstanding her Agrarian, submitted her neck to the arbitrary yoke of her princes.[4]

[2] Aristotle *Politics* 2.7. 1266b ff.

[3] Machiavelli, *Discourses*, I, 37.

[4] I Sam. 8:4-22. "But the people refused to hearken unto the voice of Samuel; and they said: 'Nay; but there shall be a king over us; that we also may be like all the nations. . . .'" (Verses 19-20). Harrington found this event difficult to explain in terms of his theory.

"4. Wherefore to come to my fourth assertion that it is destructive to families, this also is so apparent that it needs pity rather than proof. Why, alas, do you bind a nobility, which no generation shall deny to have been the first that freely sacrificed her blood to the ancient liberties of this people, upon an unholy altar? Why are the people taught that their liberty, which except our noble ancestors had been born must have long since been buried, cannot now be born except *we* be buried? A commonwealth should have the innocence of the dove—let us leave this purchase of her birth unto the serpent, which eats herself out of the womb of her mother.

"5. But it may be said perhaps that we are fallen from our first love, become proud and idle. It is certain, my Lords, that the hand of God is not upon us for nothing; but take heed how you admit of such assaults and sallies upon men's estates as may slacken the nerve of labor and give others also reason to believe that their sweat is vain or, whatsoever be pretended, your Agrarian (which is my fifth assertion) must indeed destroy industry. For that so it did in Sparta is most apparent, as also that it could do no otherwise, where every man having his forty quarters of barley, with wine proportionable, supplied him out of his own lot by his laborer or helot, and being confined in that to the scantling above which he might not live, there was not any such thing as a trade or other art, save that of war, in exercise; wherefore a Spartan, if he were not in arms, must sit and play with his fingers, whence ensued perpetual war and, the estate of the city being as little capable of increase as that of the citizen, her inevitable ruin. Now what better ends you can propose to yourselves in like ways I do not so well see as that there may be worse; for Sparta yet was free from civil war, but if *you* employ your citizens no better than she did I cannot promise that you shall fare so well because both they are still desirous of war that hope it may be profitable to them and the strongest security you can give of peace is to make it gainful, otherwise men will rather choose that whereby they may break your laws than that whereby your laws may break them; of which I do not speak so much in relation to the nobility, or such as would be holding, as to the people or them that would be getting, the passion in these being of so much the more strength, as a man's felicity is weaker in the fruition of things than in the prosecution and increase of them.

"Truly, my Lords, it is my fear that by taking off more hands, and the best, from industry you will farther damage it than can be repaired by laying on a few and the worst, while the nobility must be forced to send their sons to the plough and, as if this were not enough, to marry their daughters also to farmers.

"6. But I do not see (to come to the last point) how it is possible that this thing should be brought about—to your good I mean, though it may to the destruction of many; for that the Agrarian of Israel or that of Sparta might stand is no such miracle, the lands, without any consideration of the former proprietor, being surveyed and cast into equal lots which could neither be bought nor sold nor multiplied, so that they knew whereabout to have a man; but in this nation no such division can be introduced, the lands being already in the hands of proprietors and such whose estates lie very rarely together but mixed one with another, being also of tenures in nature so different, that as there is no experience that an Agrarian was ever introduced in such a case, so there is no appearance how or reason why it should—but that which is against reason and experience is impossible."

The case of my Lord Philautus was the most concerned in the whole nation, for he had four younger brothers, his father being yet living unto whom he was heir of ten thousand pounds a year; wherefore being a man both of good parts and esteem, his words wrought both upon men's reason and passions and had borne a stroke at the head of the business if my Lord Archon had not interposed the buckler in this oration:

"My Lords, the Legislators of Oceana: My Lord Philautus has made a thing which is easy seem hard—if he owed the thanks to his eloquence, it would be worthy of less praise than that he owes it to his merit and the love that he has most deservedly purchased of all men; nor is it rationally to be feared that he who is so much beforehand in his private should be in arrear in his public capacity. Wherefore my Lord's tenderness throughout his speech arising from no other principle than his solicitude lest the Agrarian should be hurtful to his country, it is no less than my duty to give the best satisfaction I am able to so good a patriot, taking every one of his doubts in the order proposed: and,

"1. First, whereas my Lord upon observation of the modern commonwealths is of the opinion that an Agrarian is not necessary, it must be confessed that at the first sight of them there is some appearance favoring his assertion, but upon accidents of no precedent to us. For the commonwealths of Switzerland and Holland, I mean of those Leagues being situated in countries not alluring the inhabitants to wantonness but obliging them to universal industry, have an implicit Agrarian in the nature of them and, being not obnoxious [5] to a growing nobility (which as long as their former monarchies had spread the wing over them could either not at all be hatched or was soon broken), are of no example to us, whose experience in this point has been to the contrary. But what if even in these governments there be indeed an explicit Agrarian? For when the law commands an equal or near equal distribution of a man's estate in land among his children, as in those countries, a nobility cannot grow, and so there needs no Agrarian or is one. And for the growth of the nobility in Venice (if so it be, for Machiavelli observes in that republic, as a cause of it, a great mediocrity of estates),[6] it is not a point that she is to fear but might study, seeing she consists of nothing else but nobility, by which whatever their estates suck from the people, especially if it come equally, is digested into the better blood of that commonwealth, which is all, or the greatest benefit they can have by accumulation;

5 See note 6, p. 23.
6 *Discourses*, I, 55.

for how unequal soever you will have them to be in their incomes, they have Officers of the Pomp [7] to bring them equal in expenses or at least in the ostentation or show of them. And so unless the advantage of an estate consist more in the measure than in the use of it, the authority of Venice but enforces our Agrarian, nor shall a man evade or elude the prudence of it by the authority of any other commonwealth, for if a commonwealth have been introduced at once, as those of Israel and Sparta, you are certain to find her underlaid with this as the main foundation; nor if she have owed more to fortune than prudence has she raised her head without musing upon this matter, as appears by that of Athens, which through her defect in this point, says Aristotle, introduced her ostracism, as most of the democracies of Greece. *'Ob hanc itaque causam civitates quae democratice administrantur ostracismum instituunt':* [8] But not to restrain a fundamental of such latitude to any one kind of government. Do we not yet see that if there be a sole landlord of a vast territory, he is the Turk? That if a few landlords overbalance a populous country, they have store of servants? That if a people be in equal balance, they can have no lords? That no government can otherwise be erected than upon some one of these foundations? That no one of these foundations (each being else apt to change into some other) can give any security to the government unless it be fixed? That through the want of this fixation, potent monarchies and commonwealths have fallen upon the heads of the people and accompanied their own sad ruins with vast effusions of innocent blood? Let the fame, as was the merit, of the ancient nobility of this nation be equal to or above what has been already said or can be spoken, yet have we seen not only their glory but that of a throne, the

[7] The *Proveditori alle pompe* were Venetian magistrates charged with the responsibility of preventing the spread of luxury in the republic. For further discussion, see *Oceana* (Liljegren), p. 299.

[8] "Reasons of this nature will serve to explain why democratic states institute the rule of ostracism." Aristotle *Politics* iii. 13. 1284a (Barker's translation).

most indulgent to and the least invasive for so many ages upon the liberty of a people that the world has known, through the mere want of fixing her foot by a proportionable Agrarian upon her proper foundation to have fallen with such horror as has been a spectacle of astonishment to the whole earth. And were it well argued from one calamity that we ought not to prevent another? Nor is Aristotle so good a commonwealthsman for deriding the invention of Phaleas, as in recollecting himself where he says that democracies, where a lesser part of their citizens overtop the rest in wealth, degenerate into oligarchies and principalities and, which comes nearer to the present purpose, that the greater part of the nobility of Tarantum coming accidentally to be ruined, the government of the few came by consequence to be changed into that of the many.[9]

"These things considered, I cannot see how an Agrarian as to the fixation or security of a government can be less than necessary. And if the cure be necessary, it excuses not the patient, his disease being otherwise desperate, that it is dangerous; which was the case of Rome, not so stated by Machiavelli, where he says 'that the strife about the Agrarian caused the destruction of that commonwealth.' [10] As if when a senator was not rich (as Crassus held) except he could pay an army, that commonwealth could have done other than ruin, whether in strife about the Agrarian, or without it: *'Nuper divitiae avaritiam et abundantes voluptates desiderium per luxum atque libidinem pereundi perdendique omnia invexere.'* [11] If the greatest security of a commonwealth consists in being provided with the proper antidote against this poison, her greatest danger must be from the absence of an Agrarian, which is the whole truth of the Roman example; for the Spartan, I shall reserve the further explication of it, as my Lord also did, to another place, and first see whether an Agrarian proportioned

[9] *Politics* v. 3. 1302b-1303a.

[10] *Discourses*, I, 37.

[11] "Recently, indeed, opulence has introduced a greediness for gain and the boundless variety of dissolute pleasures has created, in many, a passion for ruining themselves and all around them." Livy, Preface to i.

to a popular government be sufficient to keep out monarchy: my Lord is for the negative and fortified by the [example of the] people of Israel electing a king. To which I say that the action of the people therein expressed is a full answer to the objection of that example, for the monarchy neither grew upon them nor could by reason of the Agrarian possibly have invaded them if they had not pulled it upon themselves by the election of a king, which, being an accident the like whereof is not to be found in any other people so planted nor in this till as it is manifest they were given up by God to infatuation (for says He to Samuel, 'They have not rejected thee, but they have rejected Me, that I should not reign over them' [12]) has something in it which is apparent by what went before to have been besides the course of nature, and by what followed, for the king having no other foundation than the calamities of the people, so often beaten by their enemies that despairing of themselves they were contented with any change; if he had peace, as in the days of Solomon, [he] left but a slippery throne to his successor, as appeared by Rehoboam. And the Agrarian, notwithstanding the monarchy thus introduced, so faithfully preserved the root of that commonwealth that it shot oftener forth and by intervals continued longer than any other government, as may be computed from the institution of the same by Joshua one thousand four hundred and sixty-five years before Christ to the total dissolution of it, which happened in the reign of the emperor Hadrian one hundred and thirty-five years after the Incarnation. A people planted upon an equal Agrarian and holding to it, if they part with their liberty, must do it upon good will and make but a bad title of their bounty. As to instance yet further in that which is proposed by the present Order to this nation, the standard whereof is at two thousand pounds a year. The whole territory of Oceana being divided by this proportion amounts to five thousand lots. So the lands of Oceana being thus distributed, and bound to this distribution, can never fall to fewer than five thousand proprietors.

12 I Sam. 8:7.

But the five thousand proprietors so seased [13] will not agree to break the Agrarian, for that were to agree to rob one another; nor to bring in a king, because they must maintain him and can have no benefit by him; nor to exclude the people, because they can have as little by that and must spoil their militia. So the commonwealth continuing upon the balance proposed, though it should come to five thousand hands, can never alter, and that it should ever come to five thousand hands is as improbable as anything in the world that is not altogether impossible.

"My Lords, other considerations are more private: as that this Order destroys families—which is as if one should lay the ruins of some ancient castle to the herbs which do usually grow out of them—the destruction of those families being that indeed which naturally produced this Order. For we do not now argue for that which we would have, but for that which we are already possessed of, as would appear if a note were but taken of all such as have at this day above two thousand pounds a year in Oceana. If my Lord should grant (and I will put it with the most) that they who are proprietors in land exceeding this proportion exceed not three hundred, with what brow can the interest of so few be balanced with that of the whole nation? Or rather, what interest have they to put in such a balance? They would live as they have been accustomed to do; who hinders them? They would enjoy their estates; who touches them? They would dispose of what they have according to the interest of their families; it is that which we desire. A man has one son, let him be called; would he enjoy his father's estate? It is his, and his son's, and his son's sons after him. A man has five sons, let them be called; would they enjoy their father's estate? It is divided among them, for we have four votes for one in the same family and therefore this must be the interest of the family, or the family knows not her own interest. If a man shall dispute otherwise, he must draw his arguments from custom and from greatness, which was the interest of the monarchy, not of the family;

[13] Possessed.

and we are now a commonwealth. If the monarchy could not bear with such divisions because they tended to a commonwealth, neither can a commonwealth connive at such accumulations because they tend to a monarchy. If the monarchy might make bold with so many for the good of one, we may make bold with one for the good of so many, nay, for the good of all. My Lords, it comes into my head that upon occasion of the variety of parties enumerated in our late Civil Wars, [it] was said by a friend of mine coming home from his travels about the latter end of these troubles that he admired how it came to pass that younger brothers, especially being so many more in number than their elder, did not make one against a tyranny the like whereof has not been exercised in any other nation. And truly, when I consider that our countrymen are none of the worst natured, I must confess I marvel much how it comes to pass that we should use our children as we do our puppies—take one, lay it in the lap, feed it with every good bit, and drown five! Nay, worse, forasmuch as the puppies are once drowned, whereas the children are left perpetually drowning. Really, my Lords, it is a flinty custom! And all this for his cruel ambition that would raise himself a pillar—a golden pillar for his monument—though he have children, his own reviving flesh, and a kind of immortality. And this is that interest of a family for which we are to think ill of a government that will not endure it. But quiet yourselves. The land through which the river Nile wanders in one stream is barren, but where he parts into seven he multiplies his fertile shores, by distributing yet keeping and improving such a property and nutrition as is a prudent Agrarian to a well-ordered commonwealth.

"Nor (to come to the fifth assertion) is a political body rendered any fitter for industry by having one gouty and another withered leg, than a natural; it tends not to the improvement of merchandise that there be some who have no need of their trading, and others that are not able to follow it. If confinement discourage industry, an estate in money is not confined; and lest industry should want whereupon to work, land is not engrossed nor entailed upon any man, but remains at her devotion. I wonder whence the computation can arise that this should discourage industry? Two thousand pounds a year a man may enjoy in Oceana, as much in Panopea, five hundred in Marpesia; there be other plantations, and the Commonwealth will have more—who knows how far the arms of our Agrarian may extend themselves? And whether he that might have left a pillar may not leave a temple [of] many pillars unto his more pious memory? Where there is some measure in riches, a man may be rich; but if you will have them to be infinite, there will be no end of starving himself and wanting what he has—and what pains does such a one take to be poor! Furthermore, if a man shall think that there may be an industry less greasy or more noble, and so cast his thoughts upon the Commonwealth, he will have leisure for her and she riches and honors for him; his sweat shall smell like Alexander's.[14] My Lord Philautus is a young man who, enjoying his ten thousand pounds a year, may keep a noble house in the old way and have homely guests, and having but two [thousand] by the means proposed, may take the upper hand of his great ancestors, with reverence unto whom, I may say, there has not been one of them would have disputed his place with a Roman Consul. My Lord, do not break my heart; the nobility shall go unto no other ploughs than those from which we call our consuls. But, says he, it having been so with Sparta that neither the city nor the citizens was capable of increase, a blow was given by that Agrarian which ruined both. And what are we concerned with that Agrarian or that blow while our citizens and our city (and that by our Agrarian) are both capable of increase? The Spartan if he made a conquest had not citizens to hold it, the Oceaner will have enough; the Spartan could have no trade, the Oceaner may have all. The Agrarian in Sparta, that it might bind on knapsacks, forbidding all other arts but that of war, could not make an army of above thirty thousand citizens. The Agrarian in

14 For the belief that the sweat of Alexander the Great smelled sweet, see Plutarch's *Life of Alexander* iv. 2.

Oceana, without interruption of traffic, provides us in the fifth part of the youth an annual source or fresh spring of one hundred thousand, besides our provincial auxiliaries, out of which to draw marching armies, and as many elders, not feeble but men most of them in the flower of their age and in arms for the defense of our territories. The Agrarian in Sparta banished money; this multiplies it. That allowed a matter of twenty or thirty acres to a man; this, two or three thousand—there is no comparison between them. And yet I differ so much from my Lord, or his opinion that the Agrarian was the ruin of Sparta, that I hold it no less than demonstrable to have been her main support, for if banishing all other diversions it could not make an army of above thirty thousand, then letting in all other diversions it must have broken that army; wherefore Lysander, bringing in the golden spoils of Athens, irrevocably ruined that commonwealth, and is a warning to us that in giving encouragement to industry we also remember that 'covetousness is the root of all evil.' [15] And our Agrarian can never be the cause of those seditions threatened by my Lord, but is the proper cure of them, as Lucan notes well in the state of Rome before the civil wars, which happened through the want of such an antidote:

> *Hinc usura vorax, rapidumque in tempore Foenus,*
> *Hinc concussa fides, et multis utile bellum.*[16]

"Why then are we [misunderstood], as if we intended not equal advantages in our commonwealth to either sex, because we would not have women's fortunes consist in that metal which exposes them to cutpurses. If a man cut my purse, I may have him by the heels or by the neck for it; whereas a man may cut a woman's purse and have her for his pains in

[15] I Tim. 6:10.

[16] "Hence devouring usury, and the interest accumulating in lapse of time—Hence shaken credit, and warfare profitable to the many." Lucanus *Pharsalia* (or *De bello civili*) i. 158f. The words with which Harrington introduces this quotation are almost identical with those used by Bacon for the same purpose in his *Essay XV*, "Of seditions and troubles"; this would seem to indicate Bacon as the immediate source.

fetters. How brutish, and how much more than brutish, is
that commonwealth which prefers the earth before the fruits
of her womb? If the people be her treasure, the staff by which
she is sustained and comforted, with what justice can she suffer them by whom she is most enriched to be for that cause
the most impoverished? And yet we see the gifts of God and
the bounties of Heaven in fruitful families through this
wretched custom of marrying for money become their insup-
portable grief and poverty; nor falls this so heavy upon the
lower sort, being better able to shift for themselves, as upon
the nobility or gentry, for what avails it in this case from
whence their veins have derived their blood, while they shall
see the tallow of a chandler sooner converted into that beauty
which is required in a bride? I appeal whether my Lord
Philautus or myself be the advocate of nobility, against which
in the case proposed by me there would be nothing to hold
the balance. And why is a woman, if she may have but fifteen
hundred pounds, undone? If she be unmarried, what noble-
man allows his daughter in that case a greater revenue than
so much money may command? And if she marry, no noble-
man can give his daughter a greater portion than she has.
Who is hurt in this case? Nay, who is not benefited? If the
Agrarian give us the sweat of our brows without diminution,
if it prepare our table, if it make our cup to overflow, and
above all this, in providing for our children anoint our
heads with that oil which takes away the greatest of worldly
cares, what man that is not besotted with a covetousness as
vain as [it is] endless can imagine such a constitution to be
his poverty, seeing [that] where no woman can be considerable
for her portion, no portion will be considerable with a woman:
and so his children will not only find better preferments
without his brokerage, but more freedom of their own affec-
tions. We are wonderfully severe in laws, [providing] that they
shall not marry without our consent, as if it were care and
tenderness over them. But is it not [rather] lest we should
not have the other thousand pounds with this son, or the
other hundred pounds a year more in jointure for that daugh-

ter? These, when we are crossed in them, are the sins for which we water our couch with tears—but not of penitence; seeing whereas it is a mischief beyond any that we can do to our enemies, we persist to make nothing of breaking the affection of our children. But there is in this Agrarian an homage to pure and spotless love, the consequence whereof I will not give for all your romances. An alderman makes not his daughter a countess till he have given her twenty thousand pounds, nor a romance a considerable mistress till she be a princess; these are characters of bastard love. But if our Agrarian exclude ambition and covetousness we shall at length have the care of our own breed, in which we have been curious [i.e., careful] as to that of our dogs and our horses. The marriage bed will be truly legitimate and the race of the commonwealth not spurious.

"But *(impar magnanimis ausis imparque dolori)*[17] I am hurled from all my hopes by my Lord's last assertion of impossibility that the root from whence we imagine these fruits should be planted or thrive in this soil. And why? Because of the mixture of estates and variety of tenures. Nevertheless there is still extant in the Exchequer an old survey of the whole nation,[18] wherefore such a thing is not impossible. Now if a new survey were taken at the present rates and the law made that no man should hold hereafter above so much land as is valued therein at two thousand pounds a year, it would amount to a good and sufficient Agrarian. It is true that there would remain some difficulty in the different kind of rents, and that it is a matter requiring not only more leisure than we have, but an authority which may be better able to bow men to a more general consent than is to be wrought out of them by such as are in our capacity. Wherefore, as to the manner, it is necessary that we refer it to the parliament; but

---

[17] "Unequal to glorious deeds and unequal to pain." An alternate reading would be, "unequal to glorious deeds and unequal to trickery," assuming that *dolori* is a misprint for *dolosis.*

[18] Harrington refers to the Domesday survey of William I and the two volumes of the Domesday Book.

as to the matter, they can no otherwise fix their government upon the right balance.

"I shall conclude with a few words to some parts of the Order which my Lord has omitted. As first to the consequences of the Agrarian to be settled in Marpesia [Scotland], which irreparably breaks the aristocracy of that nation [which is] of such a nature as standing [that] it is not possible that you should govern. For while the people of that country are little better than the cattle of the nobility, you must not wonder if according as these can make their markets with foreign princes, you find those to be driven upon your grounds.[19] And if you be so tender now [when] you have it in your power, as not to hold a hand upon them that may prevent the slaughter that must otherwise ensue in like cases, the blood will lie at your door. But in holding such a hand upon them you may settle the Agrarian; and in settling the Agrarian, you give the people not only liberty but lands, which makes your protection necessary to their security, and their contribution due to your protection as to their own safety.

"For the Agrarian of Panopea [Ireland], it allowing such proportions of so good land, men that conceive themselves straitened by this in Oceana will begin there to let themselves forth, where every citizen will in time have his villa. And there is no question but the improvement of that country by this means must be far greater than it has been in the best of former times.

"I have no more to say but that in those ancient and heroical ages, when men thought that to be necessary which was virtuous, the nobility of Athens having the people so much engaged in their debt that there remained no other question among these than which of those should be king, no sooner [had the nobility] heard Solon speak than they quitted their debts and restored the commonwealth, which ever after held a solemn and annual feast called the *Sisacthia* (or Recision)

---

[19] Harrington here alludes to the use of Scottish troops in England, which he blames on the power of the Scottish nobility and the poverty of the people of Scotland.

in memory of that action.[20] Nor is this example the phoenix; for at the institution by Lycurgus, the nobility having estates (as ours here) in the lands of Sparta, upon no other valuable consideration than the commonwealth proposed by him, threw them up to be parceled by his Agrarian. But now, when no man is desired to throw up a farthing of his money or a shovel full of his earth, and all that we can do is but to make a virtue of necessity, we are disputing whether we should have peace or war. For peace you cannot have without some government, nor any government without the proper balance. Wherefore if you will not fix this which you have, the rest is blood, for without blood you can bring in no other."

By these speeches, made at the institution of the Agrarian, you may perceive what were the grounds of it.

III

Speech of the Lord Archon
Concerning the Senate of Oceana

The following selection, like the previous one, is taken from the third part of the *Oceana*, "The Model of the Commonwealth of Oceana." It consists of one of the many speeches attributed to the Lord Archon, Olphaus Megaletor, in the Council of Legislators of Oceana. The Lord Archon is commenting on, and justifying, the twentieth Order of the Oceanic constitution—the Order which explains the functioning of the Senate and its councils, in Harrington's words, "implicitly containing the sum very near of the whole civil part of the Commonwealth." The speech contains Harrington's best discussion of the political role of a nobility in a commonwealth, one of the most important features of his general theory. This selection is found on pp. 142-155 of the first edition of *Oceana;* pp. 117-127 of Liljegren's edition.

[20] See Plutarch's *Life of Solon* xiv and xv. 3.

"My Dear Lords, there is a saying that a man must cut his coat according to his cloth. When I consider what God has allowed or furnished to our present work I am amazed. You would have a popular government; he has weighed it unto you in the present balance as I may say, to a dram; you have no more to do, but to fix it. For the superstructures of such a government, they require a good Aristocracy; you have, or have had, a nobility or gentry the best studied and the best writers (at least next that of Italy) in the whole world; nor have they been inferior, when so exercised, in the leading of armies. But the people are the main body of a commonwealth; show me *(a Gadibus usque Auroram et Gangem)* from the treasuries of snow (as it is in Job) unto the burning zone a people whose shoulders so universally and so exactly fit the corselet.[1] Nevertheless, it were convenient to be well provided with auxiliaries; there is Marpesia, through her fruitfulness inexhaustible of men, and men [who are] through her barrenness not only inured to hardship but bucked in your arms. It may be said that Venice, save only that she takes not in the people,[2] is the most incomparable situation of a commonwealth. You are Venice taking in your people and your auxiliaries too. My Lords, the children of Israel were makers of brick before they were builders of a commonwealth,[3] but our brick is made, our mortar tempered, the cedars of Lebanon are hewed and squared unto our hands. Has this been the work of man? Or is it in man to withstand this work? 'Shall he that contendeth with the Almighty instruct him? He that reproveth God, let him answer it.'[4] For our parts everything is so laid that when we come to have use of it, it is the next at hand, and unless we can conceive that God

1 ". . . from Gades to the Ganges and the morn." That is, from one end of one end of the earth to the other. See Juvenal *Satire* X. 1. Also, Job 38:22.

2 For Harrington's argument that Venice was a democratic commonwealth despite the exclusion of most of the population from political activity see p. 52.

3 Exod. 5:7ff.

4 Job 40:2.

and nature do anything in vain, there is no more for us to do but to dispatch. The piece which we have reached to us in the foregoing Orders is the Aristocracy. Athens, as has been shown, was plainly lost through the want of a good aristocracy; but the sufficiency of an aristocracy goes demonstrably upon the hand of the nobility or gentry, for that the politics can be mastered without study, or that the people can have leisure to study, is a vain imagination. And what kind of aristocracy divines and lawyers would make, let their incurable run upon their own narrow bias and their perpetual invectives against Machiavelli (though in some places justly reprovable, yet the only politician and incomparable patron of the people) serve for instruction. I will stand no more unto the judgment of lawyers and divines in this work than unto that of so many other tradesmen. But if this Model chance to wander abroad, I recommend it to the Roman *Speculativi* *(Garbatissimi Signori)*, the most complete gentlemen of this age,[5] for their censure. Or, with my Lord Epimonus' leave,[6] send three or four hundred copies to your agent at Venice to be presented to the magistrates there and, when they have considered them, to be proposed to the debate of the Senate [of Venice], the most competent judges under Heaven, who though they have great affairs will not refuse to return you the oracle of their ballot. The counselors of princes I will not trust; they are but journeymen. 'The wisdom of these later times in Princes' affairs,' says Verulamius,[7] 'is rather fine deliveries and shiftings off dangers when they be near than

[5] Although this appears to be a reference to some particular body of Roman gentlemen, in all probability Harrington is simply alluding to the general reputation of the Italians in the seventeenth century. Liljegren cites James Howell's statement in his *Forren Travell* (1642), "The Italians are for the most part of a speculative complexion."

[6] Epimonus de Garrula (from the Greek meaning "prolonged" and the Latin meaning "verbose") had delivered a speech earlier in the *Oceana* ridiculing the Venetian system of ballots. As Harrington noted in *Oceana*, p. 118: "Never was there goose so stuck with lard as my Lord Epimonus's speech with laughter."

[7] Francis Bacon, *Essay XIX*, "Of Empire."

solid and grounded courses to keep them aloof.' Their counselors do not derive their proceedings from any sound root
of government, that may contain the demonstration and as-
sure the success of them, but are expedient-mongers, givers
of themselves to help a lame dog over a stile. Else how comes
it to pass that the fame of Cardinal Richelieu has been like
thunder, whereof we hear the noise but can make no demonstration of the reason? But to return, if neither the people,
nor divines and lawyers, can be the aristocracy of a nation
there remains only the Nobility, in which style, to avoid further repetition, I shall understand the gentry also, as the
French do by the word *noblesse*.

"Now to treat of the nobility, in such sort as may be less
obnoxious to mistake, it will be convenient and responsible
to the present occasion that I divide my discourse into four
Parts:

> *The first treating of* Nobility, *and the kinds of it;*
> *The second, of their capacity of the* Senate;
> *The third, of the divers kinds of* Senates;
> *The fourth, of the* Senate, *according unto the foregoing*
> *Orders.*

"Nobility may be defined divers ways, for it is either ancient riches, or ancient virtue, or title conferred by a prince
or a commonwealth.

"Nobility of the first kind may be subdivided into two
other: such as hold an overbalance in dominion or property
to the whole people, or such as hold not an overbalance. In
the former case a nobility (such was the Gothic, of which sufficient has been spoken) is incompatible with popular government. For to popular government it is essential that the power
should be in the people, but the overbalance of a nobility in
dominion draws the power to themselves. Wherefore in this
sense it is that Machiavelli is to be understood where he says,
(*'Questi tali sono pernitiosi in ogni Republica e in ogni pro-
vincia'*) that these are pernicious in a commonwealth, and of
France, Spain and Italy that they are nations (*'lequali tutte*

inscieme sono la corruttela del mondo') which for this cause
are the corruption of the world.[8] For otherwise nobility may
according to his definition, which is that 'they are such as live
upon their own revenues in plenty, without engagement either
to the tilling of their lands or other work for their livelihood,'
hold an underbalance to the people; in which case they are
not only safe but necessary to the natural mixture of a well-
ordered commonwealth.[9] For how else can you have a commonwealth that is not altogether mechanical? Or what comparison is there of such commonwealths as are or come nearest to [being] mechanical (for example Athens, Switzerland,
Holland) to Sparta, Rome, and Venice, plumed with their
aristocracies? [10] Your mechanics, till they have first feathered
their nests, like the fowls of the air whose whole employment
is to seek their food, are so busied in their private concern-
ments that they have neither leisure to study the public nor
are safely to be trusted with it (*'quia egestas haud facile habe-
tur sine damno'*) [11] because a man is not faithfully embarked
in this kind of ship if he have no share in the freight. But if
his share be such as gives him leisure by his private advantage
to reflect upon that of the public, what other name is there
for this sort of men (being *à leur aise*) but (as Machiavelli you
see calls them) nobility? Especially when their families come
to be such as are noted for their services done to the commonwealth, and so take into their ancient riches ancient virtue,
which is the second definition of nobility, but such a one as
is scarce possible in nature without the former. 'For as the
baggage,' says Verulamius,[12] 'is to an army, so are riches to
virtue; they cannot be spared nor left behind, though they

[8] *Discourses*, I, 55.

[9] See *loc. cit.* for Machiavelli's definition.

[10] By "mechanical," Harrington means populated by manual laborers.
See Aristotle's *Politics* iii. 5, for a discussion of the civic capabilities of
"mechanics."

[11] "Scarce any need is to be sustained without damage." Liljegren attributes this quotation to Julius Exsuperantius, a Latin historian of the fourth
century, author of *De Marii, Lepidi & Sertorii bellis civilibus*.

[12] Bacon, *Essay XXXIV*, "Of Riches."

be *impedimenta*—such as not only hinder the march but sometimes through the care of them lose or disturb the victory.' Of this latter sort is the nobility of Oceana, the best of all others because they, having no stamp whence to derive their price, can have it no otherwise than by their intrinsic value. The third definition of nobility is title, honor, or distinction from the people, conferred or allowed by the prince or the commonwealth. And this may be in two ways, either without any stamp or privilege as in Oceana, or with such privileges as are inconsiderable, as in Athens after the battle of Plataea,[13] whence the nobility had no right as such [except] unto religious offices or inspection of the public games, whereunto they were also to be elected by the people; or [the second way] with privileges, and those considerable ones, as the nobility in Athens before the battle of Plataea and the patricians in Rome, each of which had right, or claimed it, to the senate and all the magistracies, wherein for some time they only by their stamp were current.

"But to begin higher and speak more at large of nobility in their several capacities of the senate: *(a Jove Principium)* [14] the phylarchs or princes of the Tribes of Israel were the most renowned or, as the Latin [has it], the most noble of the Congregation, (Num. 1:16) whereof by hereditary right they had the leading and judging. The patriarchs or princes of families according as they declared their pedigrees (Num. 1:18) had the like rights as to their families, but neither in these nor the former was there any hereditary right to the *Sanhedrin*. Though there be little question but the wise men, and understanding and known among their Tribes which the people took or elected into those or other magistracies, and Moses made rulers over them (Deut. 1:13) must have been of these, seeing these could not choose but be the most known among the Tribes and were likeliest by the advantages of education to be the most wise and understanding.

[13] The Greeks, under the Spartan Pausanius, defeated a Persian army at Plataea in the year 479 B.C.

[14] "To begin with Jove . . ." See Virgil *Bucolics* iii. 60.

"Solon, having found the Athenians neither locally nor genealogically, but [rather] by their different ways of life divided into four tribes—that is, into the soldiery, the tradesmen, the husbandmen, and the goatherds—instituted a new distribution of them according to the census, or evaluation of their estates, into four classes. The first, second, and third, consisting of such as were proprietors in land distinguished by the rate of their freeholds, with that stamp upon them which making them capable of honor unto their riches (that is to say, of the senate and all the magistracies), excluded the fourth (being the body of the people and far greater in number than the former three) from other right as to those capacities than the election of [the first three classes] who, by this means, became an hereditary aristocracy or senatorian order of nobility. This was that course which came afterwards to be the destruction of Rome and had now ruined Athens (the nobility, according to the inevitable nature of such a one, having laid the plot how to divest the people of the result and so draw the whole power of the commonwealth to themselves, which in all likelihood they had done) if the people, coming by mere chance to be victorious in the battle of Plataea and famous for defending Greece against the Persian, had not returned with such courage as irresistibly broke the classes (to which of old they had borne a white tooth), brought the nobility to equal terms and the Senate with the magistracies to be common to both—the magistracies by suffrage and the Senate, which was the mischief of it as I shall show anon in that constitution, by lot only.

"The Spartans were in the manner, and for the same cause with the Venetians at this day, no other than nobility, even according to the definition of nobility given by Machiavelli, for they neither exercised any trade nor labored their lands or lots, which was done by their helots. Wherefore some nobility may be far from pernicious in a commonwealth, by Machiavelli's own testimony, who is an admirer of this [Spartan commonwealth], though the servants thereof were more [numerous] than the citizens. To these servants, I hold the answer of Lycurgus,[15] when he bade him who asked why he did not admit the people to the government of his commonwealth go home and admit his servants to the government of his family, to relate; for neither were the Spartans servants, nor further capable of the government, unless, whereas the congregation had the result, he should have given them the debate also; every one of these that attained to sixty years of age, and the major vote of the congregation, being equally capable of [election to] the Senate.

"The nobility of Rome and their capacity of the Senate I have already described by that of Athens before the battle of Plataea, save only that the Athenian was never eligible into the Senate without the suffrage of the people till the introduction of the lot, but the Roman nobility [was] ever; for the patricians were elected into the Senate by the Kings, by the Consuls, or the Censors; or if a plebeian happened to be conscribed, he and his posterity became patrician. Nor, though the people had many disputes with the nobility, did this ever come in controversy, which if there had been nothing else might in my judgment have been enough to overturn that commonwealth.

"The Venetian nobility, but that they are richer and not military, resemble at all other points the Spartan, as I have already shown. These Machiavelli excepts from his rule by saying that their estates are rather personal than real or of any great revenue in land. Which comes to our account and shows that a nobility or party of the nobility not overbalancing in dominion is not dangerous, but of necessary use in every commonwealth, provided that it be rightly ordered. For if it be so ordered as was that of Rome, though they do not overbalance in the beginning, as they did not there, it will not be long ere they do, as is clear both in reason and that experience towards the later end. That the nobility only be capable of the Senate is there only not dangerous where there be no other citizens, as in this government [of Venice] and that of Sparta.

15 Plutarch *Lycurgus* xix. 6.

"The nobility of Holland and Switzerland, though but few, have privileges not only distinct from the people, but so great that in some sovereignties they have a negative voice—an example which I am far from commending, being such as if those governments were not cantonized, divided, and subdivided into many petty sovereignties that balance one another, and in which the nobility except they had a prince at the head of them can never join to make work, would be the most dangerous that ever was, [except] the Gothic, of which it savors. For in ancient commonwealths you shall never find a nobility to have had a negative but by the poll, which, the people being far more in number, came to nothing; whereas these have it, be they never so few, by their stamp or order.

"Ours of Oceana have nothing else but their education and their leisure for the public, furnished by their ease and competent riches, and their intrinsic value, which according as it comes to hold weight in the judgment or suffrage of the people is their only way to honor and preferment. Wherefore I would have your Lordships to look upon your children as such who, if they come to shake off some part of their baggage, shall make the more quick and glorious march; for it was nothing else but the baggage sordidly plundered by the nobility of Rome that lost the victory of the whole world in the midst of her triumph.

"Having followed the nobility thus close, they bring us, according to their natural course and divers kind, to the divers constitutions of the senate.

"That of Israel (as was shown by my right noble Lord Phosphorus de Auge in the opening of the commonwealth) consisted of seventy elders, elected at first by the people. But whereas they were [elected] for life, they ever after (though without any divine precept for it) substituted their successors by ordination, which ceremony was most usually performed by the imposition of hands, and by this means a commonwealth of as popular institution as can be found became, as it is accounted by Josephus,[16] aristocratical. From this ordina-

[16] Josephus *Antiquitatis Judaicae* xi. 4.8 and *De bello Judaico* i. 8.5.

tion derives that which was introduced by the Apostles into
the Christian Church; for which cause I think it is that the
Presbyterians would have the government of the Church to
be aristocratical, albeit the Apostles, to the end, as I conceive,
that they might give no occasion to such a mistake but show
that they intended the government of the Church to be popular, ordained elders (as has been shown) by the holding up of
hands (or free suffrage of the people) in every congregation
or *ecclesia,* for that is the word in the original, being borrowed
from the civil congregation of the people in Athens and Sparta,
which were so called. And the word for 'holding up of hands'
in the text is also the very same which signified the suffrage
of the people in Athens, χειροτονήσαντες; for the suffrage of
the Athenians was given *per* χειροτονίαν, says Emmius.[17]

"The Council of the Bean (as was shown by my Lord
Navarchus de Paralo in his full discourse) being the proposing senate of Athens (for that of the Areopagites was a judicatory) consisted of four, some say five, hundred senators
elected annually all at once, and by a mere lot without suffrage. Wherefore albeit the senate, to correct the temerity of
the lot, had power to cast out such as they should judge un-
worthy of that honor, this related to manners only and was
not sufficient to repair the commonwealth, which by such
means became impotent; and for as much as her senate consisted not of the natural aristocracy, which in a commonwealth
is the only spur and rein of the people, [Athens] was cast
headlong by the rashness of her demagogues or grandees into
ruin; while her senate, like the Roman tribunes (*"qui fere
semper regebantur a multitudine magis quam regebant"*),[18]
proposed not to the result only, but to the debate also of the
people, who were therefore called to the pulpits, where some
vomited and others drank poison.

"The Senate of Sparta (most truly discovered by my Lord
Laco de Scytale) consisted of 30 for life, whereof the two

17 Ubbo Emmius, *Graecorum res publicae* (1632), p. 43.
18 "[The Tribunes] in every case are rather ruled by, than rule the
multitude. . . ." Livy, iii. 71.

Kings having but single votes were hereditary, the rest elective by the free suffrage of the people, but [only] out of such as were sixty years of age. These [senators] had the whole debate of the commonwealth in themselves and proposed to the result only of the people. And now the riddle which I have heretofore found troublesome to unfold is out; that is to say, why Athens and Sparta consisting each of the senate and the people, the one should be held a democracy and the other an aristocracy, or laudable oligarchy, as it is termed by Isocrates,[19] (for that word is not wherever you meet it to be branded, seeing it is used also by Aristotle, Plutarch, and others, sometimes in a good sense).[20] The main difference was that the people in this [Sparta] had the result only, and in that [Athens] the debate and the result too. But for my part, where the people have the election of the senate, not bound to a distinct order, and the result which is the sovereign power, I hold them to have that share in the government (the senate being not for life) whereof, with the safety of the commonwealth, they are capable in nature, and [I hold] such a government for that cause to be democracy; though I do not deny [that] in Sparta, the paucity of the senators considered, it might be called oligarchy in comparison of Athens; or, if we look upon their continuance for life, though they had been more, aristocracy.

"The Senate of Rome (whose fame has been heard to thunder in the eloquence of my Lord Dolabella d'Enyo) consisting of three hundred was in regard of the number less oligarchical than that of Sparta, but more in regard of the patricians, who having an hereditary capacity of the same were not elected to that honor by the people, but being conscribed by the Censors enjoyed it for life. Wherefore these, if they had had their wills, would have resolved as well as debated; which set the people at such variance with them as dissolved the com-

[19] Isocrates *Nicocles*, xxiv; Harrington, however, took the quotation from Nicholas Cragius, *De republica Lacedemoniorum* (1593), p. 14.

[20] Here, again, Harrington follows Cragius, *loc. cit.* Aristotle *Politics*, iii. 7, 9, and Plutarch's *Life of Homer* may be cited as examples.

monwealth; whereas if the people had enjoyed the result, as well that [strife] about the Agrarian as all other strife must of necessity have ceased.

"The senates of Switzerland and Holland (as I have learned of my Lords Alpester and Glaucus) being bound up, like the sheaf of arrows which this gives, by leagues, lie like those in their quivers. But arrows when they come to be drawn fly some this way and some that. And I am contented that these concern us not.

"That of Venice (by the faithful testimony of my most excellent Lord Linceus de Stella) has obliged a world sufficiently punished by its own blindness or ingratitude to repent and be wiser. For whereas a commonwealth in which there is no senate, or in which the senate is corrupt, cannot stand, the Great Council of Venice like the statue of Nilus [21] leans upon an urn or waterpot, which pours forth the senate in so pure and perpetual a stream as, being unable to stagnate, is for ever incapable of corruption. The fuller description of this senate is contained in that of Oceana; and that of Oceana in the foregoing orders.[22] Unto every one of which, because something has already been said, I shall not speak in particular. But in general, your Senate (and the other assembly, or the Prerogative, as I shall show in due place) are perpetual, not as lakes or puddles, but as the rivers of Eden; [23] and are beds made, as you have seen, to receive the whole people by a due and faithful vicissitude into their current. They are not, as in the late way, alternate. Alternate life in government is the alternate death of it.

Ut fratrem Pollux alterna morte redemit.[24]

[21] Nilus was the god of the river Nile, the son of Oceanus (or Chronos). He was often pictured with an urn or water jar from which the river poured forth.

[22] Orders XV-XX of the Constitution of Oceana deal with the composition and functioning of the Senate and its councils; see *Oceana* (Liljegren), pp. 123-141.

[23] Gen. 2:10ff.

[24] "If Pollux, dying in turn, redeemed his brother . . ." Virgil *Aeneid* vi. 121.

"This was the Gothic work, whereby the former government was not only a ship, but a gust [of wind] too, could never open her sails but in danger to overset herself, neither make any voyage nor lie safe in her own harbor. The wars of later ages (says Verulamius) [25] seem to be made in the dark, in respect of the glory and honor which reflected upon men from the wars in ancient times. Their shipping of this sort was for voyages, ours dare not launch, nor lies it safe at home. Your Gothic politicians seem to me rather to have invented some new ammunition or gunpowder in their king and parliament *("duo fulmina belli")* [26] than government. For what is become of the princes (a kind of people) in Germany? Blown up. Where are the estates or the power of the people in France? Blown up. Where is that of the people in Aragon and the rest of the Spanish kingdoms? Blown up. On the other side, where is the king of Spain's power in Holland? Blown up. Where is that of the Austrian princes in Switzerland? Blown up. This perpetual peevishness and jealousy, under the alternate empire of the prince and of the people, is obnoxious [27] to every spark. Nor shall any man show a reason that will be holding in prudence why the people of Oceana have blown up their king, but that their kings did not first blow them up. The rest is discourse for ladies. Wherefore your parliaments are not henceforth to come out of the bag of Aeolus [except] by your galaxies,[28] to be the perpetual food of the fire of Vesta.

"Your galaxies which divide the House into so many regions are three, one of which constituting the third region is annually chosen, but for the term of three years; which causes the house having blooms, fruit half ripe, and others dropping off in full maturity, to resemble an orange tree—such as is at the same time an education or spring, and an harvest too.

[25] Bacon, *De augmentis scientiarum* (Frankfurt, 1665), p. 240.

[26] Virgil uses this phrase, "two thunderbolts in war," to describe the Gracchi, *Aeneid* vi. 843.

[27] See note 6, p. 23.

[28] Harrington uses the word "galaxy" to describe the list of knights and deputies elected from each Tribe to serve in the legislature of Oceana; see Order XII, *Oceana* (Liljegren), pp. 78f.

For the people have made a very ill choice in the man who is not easily capable of the perfect knowledge in one year of the senatorian orders, which knowledge allowing him for the first to have been a novice, brings him the second year to practice, and time enough. For at this rate you must always have two hundred knowing men in the government, and thus the vicissitude of your senators is not perceivable in the steadiness and perpetuity of your Senate, which, like that of Venice, being always changing, is forever the same. And though other politicians have not so well imitated their pattern, there is nothing more obvious in nature, seeing a man who wears the same flesh but a short time is nevertheless the same man and of the same genius; and whence is this but from the constancy of nature in holding a man unto her Orders? Wherefore hold also unto your Orders; but this is a mean request, your Orders will be worth little if they do not hold you unto them—wherefore embark. They are like a ship, if you be once aboard you do not carry them, but they you. And see how Venice stands unto her tackle, you will no more forsake them than you will leap into the sea.

"But they are very many, and difficult. O, my Lords, what seaman casts away his card because it has four and twenty points of the compass? And yet those are very near as many and as difficult as the Orders in the whole circumference of your commonwealth.[29] Consider how have we been tossed with every wind of doctrine, lost by the glib tongues of your demagogues and grandees, in our own havens? A company of fiddlers that have disturbed your rest for your groat; two to one, three thousand pounds a year to another, has been nothing; and for what? Is there one of them that yet knows what a commonwealth is? And are you yet afraid of such a government in which these shall not dare to scrape [their fiddles] for fear of the statute? Themistocles could not fiddle, but could make of a small city a great commonwealth;[30] these

[29] The constitution of Oceana contained thirty Orders.

[30] See Bacon, *Essay XXIX*, "Of the true greatness of kingdoms and estates." The original source is Plutarch *Themistocles* ii. 4.

have fiddled, and for your money, till they have brought a great commonwealth to a small city.

"It grieves me, while I consider how and from what causes imaginary difficulties will be aggravated, that the foregoing Orders are not capable of any greater clearness in discourse or writing. But if a man should make a book describing every trick or passage it would fare no otherwise with a game at cards; and this is no more, if a man play upon the square. 'There is a great difference,' says Verulamius,[31] 'between a cunning man and a wise man (between a demagogue and a legislator) not only in point of honesty, but in point of ability. As there be [those] that can pack the cards and yet cannot play well, so there be some that are good in canvasses and factions that are otherwise weak men.' Allow me but these Orders, and let them come with their cards in their sleeves or pack if they can. 'Again,' says he, 'it is one thing to understand persons and another to understand matters, for many are perfect in men's humors that are not greatly capable of the real part of business, which is the constitution of one that has studied men more than books; but there is nothing more hurtful in a state than that cunning men pass for wise.' His words are an oracle. As Dionysius, when he could no longer exercise his tyranny among men, turned schoolmaster, that he might exercise it among boys.[32] Allow me but these Orders, and your grandees so well skilled in the baits and palates of men shall turn ratcatchers.

"And whereas councils (as is discreetly observed by the same author in his time) [33] 'are at this day in most places but familiar meetings (somewhat like the Academy of our Provosts) [34]

[31] Bacon, *Essay XXII*, "Of Cunning."

[32] Cicero *Tusculan disputations* iii. 12, 27.

[33] Bacon, *Essay XX*, "Of Counsel."

[34] The Academy of Provosts was a council of the Senate of Oceana which met every evening: ". . . all sorts of company that will repair thither for conversation or discourse, so it be upon the matter of government, news, or intelligence, or to propose any thing unto the councils, shall be freely and affably received . . . and heard in the way of civil conversation. . . ." See Orders XVI and XIX (Liljegren, pp. 125 and 130f.).

where matters are rather talked on than debated and run too swift to order an Act of Council,' give me my Orders and see if I have not trashed your demagogues.

"It is not so much my desire to return upon haunts as [it is] theirs that will not be satisfied; wherefore if notwithstanding what was said of dividing and choosing in our Preliminary discourses, men will yet be returning to the question why the Senate must be a council apart (though even in Athens, where it was of no other constitution than the popular assembly, the distinction of it from the other was never held less than necessary), this may be added to the former reasons: that if the aristocracy be not for the debate, it is for nothing; but if it be for the debate, it must have convenience for it. And what convenience is there for debate in a crowd, where there is nothing but jostling, treading upon one another, and stirring of blood, than which in this case there is nothing more dangerous? Truly, it was not ill said of my Lord Epimonus,[35] that Venice plays her game as it were at billiards or nineholes; and so may your Lordships, unless your ribs be so strong that you think better of football; for such sport is debate in a popular assembly, as, notwithstanding the distinction of the senate, was the destruction of Athens."

This speech concluded the debate which happened at the institution of the Senate . . .

[35] See note 6, p. 133.

THE ROTA
A MODEL OF A FREE STATE

THE ROTA

A MODEL OF A FREE STATE

This selection consists of the major portion of a pamphlet entitled, *The Rota: Or a Model of a Free State, or equal Commonwealth,* written late in 1659 and published in January 1660. It is included as the best short description of the system of government which Harrington proposed as a solution to England's political problems. In all essential respects the system here outlined is identical with that first presented by Harrington in 1656 in his *Oceana.* The text of the pamphlet can be found on pp. 621-632 of Harrington's *Collected Works,* third edition, London 1747.

[A MODEL IN BRIEF OF A FREE STATE]

FOR THE FORM OR MODEL IN BRIEF OF A FREE STATE OR EQUAL COMMONWEALTH. IT HAS BEEN PROPOSED IN THIS MANNER:

1. Let the whole territory of Oceana be divided as equally as may be into fifty parts or Shires.

2. Let the whole inhabitants (except women, children, and servants) be divided according to their age into Elders and Youth, and according to their estates into Horse and Foot.

3. Let all such as are eighteen years of age or upwards to thirty be accounted Youth, and all such as are thirty or upwards, be accounted Elders.

4. Let all such as have one hundred pounds a year or upwards, in lands, goods, or money, be accounted of the Horse; and all such as have under, be accounted of the Foot of the Commonwealth.

5. Let every parish in a shire elect annually the fifth Elder of the same to be for that year a Deputy of that parish; if a parish be too small, let it be laid as to this purpose to the next; and in this respect, let every part of the territory appertain to some parish.

6. Where there is but one Elder of the Horse in a parish, let him be annually eligible, without interval; where there are more Elders of the Horse, let no Deputy of the parish be re-eligible but after the interval of one year.

7. Where there be four Elders of the Horse, or more, in one and the same parish, let not under two, nor above half of them, be elected at one and the same election or time.

8. Let the Deputies thus elected at the parishes assemble annually at the capital of their shire, and let them then and there elect out of their own number two Elders of the Horse to be Knights or Senators, three Elders of the Horse and four Elders of the Foot to be the Assembly of the People, for the term of three years, enjoining an equal vacation or interval before they can be re-elected in either of these capacities.

9. Let there be elected at the same time in each shire, the first year only, two other Knights and seven other Deputies for the term of one year, and two other Knights and seven other Deputies for the term of two years, which in all constitutes the Senate of three hundred Knights and the popular Assembly of one thousand and fifty Deputies, each being upon a triennial rotation or annual change in the one-third part.

10. Let the Senate have the whole Authority or right of debating and proposing to the people; let the popular Assembly have the whole Power of Result; and let what shall be proposed by the Senate, and resolved by the popular Assembly, be the law of Oceana.

The Conclusion

Two Assemblies thus constituted must necessarily amount to the understanding and the will, to the wisdom and the interest of the whole nation; and a commonwealth where the wisdom of the nation proposes, and the interest of the people resolves, can never fail in whatever shall be further necessary for the right constituting of itself.

THE MODEL AT LARGE OF A FREE STATE OR
EQUAL COMMONWEALTH

PROPOSED IN FOUR PARTS: FIRST, THE CIVIL; SECONDLY, THE RELIGIOUS; THIRDLY, THE MILITARY; FOURTHLY, THE PROVINCIAL.

I. For the Civil Part, it is proposed:

1. That the whole native or proper territory of Oceana (respect had to the tax roll, to the number of people, and to the extent of territory) be cast with as much exactness as can be convenient into fifty precincts, shires, or tribes.

2. That all citizens, that is, freemen, or such as are not servants, be distributed into Horse and Foot, that such of them as have one hundred pounds a year in lands, goods, or money, or above that proportion, be accounted of the Horse; and all such as have under that proportion, be accounted of the Foot.

3. That all Elders or freemen, being thirty years of age or upwards, be capable of civil administration; and that the Youth, or such freemen as are between eighteen years of age and thirty, be not capable of civil administration, but of military only, in such manner as shall follow in the military part of this Model.

4. That the Elders resident in each Parish annually assemble in the same, as for example, upon Monday next ensuing the last of December; that they then and there elect out of their own number every fifth man, or one man out of every five, to be for the term of the year ensuing a Deputy of that Parish; and that the first and second so elected be Overseers, or presidents for the regulating of all parochial congregations, whether of the Elders or of the Youth, during the term for which they were elected.

5. That so many Parishes lying nearest together, whose Deputies shall amount to one hundred, or thereabouts, be cast into one precinct called the Hundred; and that in each precinct called the Hundred, there be a town, village, or place appointed to be the capital of the same.

6. That the parochial Deputies elected throughout the Hundred assemble annually; for example, upon Monday next ensuing the last of January, at the capital of their Hundred; that they then and there elect out of the Horse of their number one Justice of the Peace, one Juryman, one Captain, one Ensign; and out of the Foot of their number, one other Juryman, one High Constable, etc.

7. That every twenty Hundreds lying nearest and most conveniently together be cast into one Tribe or Shire; that the whole territory being after this manner cast into Tribes, or Shires, some town, village, or place be appointed to every Tribe or Shire for the capital of the same; and that these three precincts—that is, the Parish, the Hundred, and the Tribe or Shire—whether the Deputies thenceforth annually chosen in the Parishes, or Hundreds, come to increase or diminish, remain firm and unalterable forever, save only by act of Parliament.

8. That the Deputies elected in the several Parishes, together with their Magistrates and other officers, both civil and military, elected in their several Hundreds, assemble or muster annually; for example, upon Monday next ensuing the last of February, at the capital of their Tribe, or Shire.

9. That the whole body thus assembled upon the first day of the assembly elect out of the Horse of their number one High Sheriff, one Lieutenant of the Tribe or Shire, one Custos Rotulorum,[1] one Conductor, and two Censors; that the High Sheriff be Commander in Chief, the Lieutenant Commander in the second place, and the Conductor in the third, of this Band, or Squadron; that the Custos Rotulorum be Mustermaster and keep the rolls; that the Censors be governors of the Ballot; and that the term of these magistracies be annual.

10. That the magistrates of the Tribe, that is to say, the High Sheriff, Lieutenant, Custos Rotulorum, the Censors, and the Conductor, together with the magistrates and officers of the Hundred, that is to say, the twenty Justices of the Peace, the forty Jurymen, the twenty High Constables, be one Troop,

[1] Keeper of the Rolls, or Records.

and one Company apart, called the Prerogative Troop or Company; that this Troop bring in and assist the Justices of Assize, hold the quarter-sessions in their several capacities, and perform their other functions as formerly.

11. That the magistrates of the Tribe or Shire, that is to say, the High Sheriff, Lieutenant, Custos Rotulorum, the Censors, and the Conductor, together with the twenty Justices elected at the Hundreds, be a court for the government of the Tribe called the Phylarch; [2] and that this court shall proceed in all matters of government as shall from time to time be directed by act of Parliament.

12. That the Squadron of the Tribe, upon the second day of their assembly, elect two Knights and three Burgesses out of the Horse of their number, and four other Burgesses out of the Foot of their number. That the Knights have session in the Senate for the term of three years, and that the Burgesses be of the Prerogative Tribe, or representative of the people, for the like term. That if in case of death or expulsion, a place become void in the Senate or popular Assembly, the respective Shire or Tribe have timely notice from the Seignory and proceed in the manner aforesaid to extraordinary election of a Deputy or Senator for the remaining part of the term of the Senator or Deputy deceased or expelled.

13. That for the full and perfect institution at once of the Assemblies mentioned, the Squadron of each Tribe or Shire, in the first year of the Commonwealth, elect two Knights for the term of one year, two other Knights for the term of two years, and lastly, two Knights more for the term of three years; the like for the Burgesses, of the Horse first and then for those of the Foot.

14. That a magistrate or officer elected at the Hundred be thereby barred from being elected a magistrate of the Tribe, or of the first day's election. That no former election whatsoever bar a man of the second day's election at the Tribe, or to be chosen a Knight or Burgess. That a man being chosen a Knight or Burgess, who before was chosen a magistrate or

2 From the Greek *"phyle,"* tribe.

officer of the Hundred or Tribe, delegate his former office or magistracy in the Hundred or the Tribe to any other Deputy, being no magistrate nor officer, and being of the same Hundred and of the same order, that is, of the Horse or of the Foot respectively. That the whole and every part of the foregoing Orders for Election in the Parishes, the Hundreds, and the Tribes be holding and inviolate upon such penalties, in case of failure, as shall hereafter be provided by act of Parliament against any Parish, Hundred, Tribe or Shire, Deputy, or person so offending.

15. That the Knights of the annual election in the Tribes take their places on Monday next ensuing the last of March in the Senate. That the like number of Knights, whose session determines [ends] at the same time, recede. That every Knight or Senator be paid out of the public revenue quarterly seventy-five pounds during his term of session, and be obliged to sit in purple robes.

16. That annually upon reception of the new Knights, the Senate proceed to election of new magistrates and counselors. That for magistrates they elect one Archon or General, one Orator or Speaker, and two Censors, each for the term of one year, these promiscuously; and that they elect one Commissioner of the Great Seal and one Commissioner of the Treasury, each for the term of three years, out of the new Knights only.

17. That the Archon or General and the Orator or Speaker, as Consuls of the Commonwealth and Presidents of the Senate, be during the term of their magistracy paid quarterly five hundred pounds; that the ensigns of these magistracies be a sword borne before the General and a mace before the Speaker; that they be obliged to wear ducal robes; and that what is said of the Archon or General in this proposition be understood only of the General sitting, and not of the General marching.

18. That the General sitting, in case he be commanded to march, receive field-pay; and that a new General be forthwith elected by the Senate to succeed him in the House, with

all the rights, ensigns, and emoluments of the General sitting; and this so often as one or more Generals are marching.

19. That the three Commissioners of the Great Seal and the three Commissioners of the Treasury, using their ensigns and habit, and performing their other functions as formerly, be paid quarterly to each of them three hundred seventy-five pounds.

20. That the Censors be each of them Chancellor of one university by virtue of their election; that they govern the ballot; that they be Presidents of the Council for Religion; that they have, under appeal to the Senate, right to note and remove a Senator that is scandalous; that each have a silver wand for the ensign of his magistracy; that each be paid quarterly three hundred seventy-five pounds, and be obliged to wear scarlet robes.

21. That the General sitting, the Speaker, and the six Commissioners aforesaid be the Seignory of this Commonwealth.[3]

22. That there be a Council of State consisting of fifteen Knights, five out of each order or election; and that the same be perpetuated by the annual election of five out of the new Knights, or last elected to the Senate.

23. That there be a Council for Religion consisting of twelve Knights, four out of each order, and perpetuated by the annual election of four out of the Knights last elected into the Senate. That there be a Council for Trade consisting of a like number, elected and perpetuated in the same manner.

24. That there be a Council of War, not elected by the Senate, but elected by the Council of State out of themselves; that this Council of War consist of nine Knights, three out of each order, and be perpetuated by the annual election of three out of the last Knights elected to the Council of State.

25. That in case the Senate add nine Knights more out of their own number to the Council of War, the said Council be understood by such addition to be Dictator of the Com-

[3] Harrington adopts the term "Seignory" from Venetian usage; as he says in the *Oceana*, "The Signory, with the whole right and use of that Magistracy, . . . is almost purely Venetian." See *Oceana* (Liljegren), p. 125.

monwealth, for the term of three months, and no longer, except by further order of the Senate the said Dictatorian power be prolonged for a like term.

26. That the Seignory have session and suffrage,[4] with right also jointly or severally to propose both in the Senate and in all Senatorian Councils.

27. That each of the three orders or divisions of Knights in each Senatorian Council elect one Provost for the term of one week; and that any two Provosts of the same Council so elected may propose to the respective Council, and not otherwise.

28. That some fair room or rooms, well furnished and attended, be allowed at the state's charge for a free and open Academy to all comers, at some convenient hour or hours toward the evening. That this Academy be governed, according to the rules of good breeding or civil conversation, by some or all of the Proposers; and that in the same it be lawful for any man by word of mouth or by writing, in jest or in earnest, to propose to the Proposers.

29. That for Ambassadors in Ordinary there be four residences, as France, Spain, Venice, and Constantinople; that every resident upon election of a new Ambassador in Ordinary remove to the next residence in the order nominated, till having served in them all, he return home. That upon Monday next ensuing the last of November, there be every second year elected by the Senate some fit person, being under thirty-five years of age, and not of the Senate nor of the popular Assembly; that the party so elected repair upon Monday next ensuing the last of March following as Ambassador in Ordinary to the Court of France, and there reside for the term of two years, to be computed from the first of April next ensuing his election. That every Ambassador in Ordinary be allowed three thousand pounds a year during the term of his residence; and that if a resident come to die, there be an extraordinary election into his residence for his term and for the remainder of his removes and progress.

---

[4] That is, the right to sit and the right to vote.

30. That all emergent elections be made by Scrutiny, that is, by a Council or by Commissioners proposing, and by the Senate resolving in the manner following: that all field officers be proposed by the Council of War; that all ambassadors extraordinary be proposed by the Council of State; that all judges and sergeants at law be proposed by the Commissioners of the Great Seal. That all barons and officers of trust in the Exchequer be proposed by the Commissioners of the Treasury; and that such as are thus proposed and approved by the Senate be held lawfully elected.

31. That the cognizance of all matter of state to be considered or law to be enacted, whether it be provincial or national, domestic or foreign, appertain to the Council of State. That such affairs of either kind as they shall judge to require more secrecy be remitted by this Council, and appertain to the Council of War, being for that end a select part of the same. That the cognizance and protection both of the national religion and of the liberty of conscience equally established, after the manner to be shown in the religious part of this model, appertain to the Council for Religion. That the matter of traffic and regulation of the same appertain to the Council for Trade. That in the exercise of these several functions, which naturally are Senatorian or authoritative only, no Council assume any other power than such only as shall be estated upon the same by act of Parliament.

32. That what shall be proposed to the Senate by one or more of the Seignory or proposers general, or whatever was proposed by any two of the Provosts or particular proposers, to their respective Council, and upon debate at that Council shall come to be proposed by the same to the Senate, be necessarily debatable and debated by the Senate. That in all cases wherein power is derived to the Senate by law made or by act of Parliament, the Result [decision] of the Senate be ultimate; that in all cases of law to be made or not already provided for by act of Parliament, as war and peace, levy of men, or money or the like, the Result of the Senate be not ultimate. That whatsoever is decreed by the Senate upon a case where

their result is not ultimate, be proposed by the Senate to the Prerogative Tribe, or representative of the people, except only in cases of such speed or secrecy wherein the Senate shall judge the necessary slowness or openness in this way of proceeding to be of detriment or danger to the Commonwealth.

33. That if upon the motion or proposition of a Council or proposer general, the Senate add nine Knights, promiscuously chosen out of their own number to the Council of War, the same Council, as thereby made Dictator, have the power of life and death, as also to enact laws in all such cases of speed or secrecy for and during the term of three months and no longer, except upon new order from the Senate; and that all laws enacted by the Dictator be good and valid for the term of one year and no longer, except the same be proposed by the Senate and resolved by the people.

34. That the Burgesses of the annual election returned by the Tribes enter into the Prerogative Tribe, popular Assembly, or representative of the people, upon Monday next ensuing the last of March; and that the like number of Burgesses, whose term is expired, recede at the same time. That the Burgesses thus entered elect to themselves out of their own number two of the Horse, one to be Captain and the other to be Cornet of the same, and two of the Foot, one to be Captain and the other to be Ensign of the same; each for the term of three years. That these officers being thus elected, the whole Tribe or Assembly proceed to the election of four annual magistrates, two out of the Foot to be Tribunes of the Foot, and two out of the Horse to be Tribunes of the Horse. That the Tribunes be Commanders of this Tribe in Chief, so far as it is a military body, and Presidents of the same, as it is a civil assembly. And lastly, that this whole Tribe be paid weekly as follows: To each of the Tribunes of the Horse, seven pounds; to each of the Tribunes of Foot, six pounds; to each of the Captains of Horse, five pounds; to each of the Captains of Foot, four pounds; to each of the Cornets, three pounds; to each of the Ensigns, two pounds,

seven shillings; to every Horseman, two pounds; and to every one of the Foot, one pound, ten shillings.

35. That inferior officers, as Captains, Cornets, Ensigns, be only for the military discipline of this Squadron or Tribe. That the Tribunes have session in the Senate without suffrage; that they have session of course and with suffrage in the Dictatorian Council, so often as it is created by the Senate. That they be Presidents of the Court in all cases to be judged by the people; and that they have right under an appeal to the popular Assembly to note or remove any Deputy or Burgess that is scandalous.

36. That peculation or defraudation of the public, all cases tending to the subversion of the government, be triable by this representative; and that there be an appeal to the same in all causes, and from all magistrates, courts, and councils, whether national or provincial.

37. That the Right of Debate, as also of proposing to the people, be wholly and only in the Senate, without any power at all of Result, not derived from the people.

38. That the power of result be wholly and only in the popular Assembly, without any right at all of Debate.

39. That the Senate, having debated and agreed upon a law to be proposed, cause promulgation of the same to be made for the space of six weeks before proposition, that is, cause the law to be printed and published so long before it is to be proposed.

40. That promulgation being made, the Seignory demand of the Tribunes being present in the Senate an Assembly of the people. That the Tribunes, upon such demand by the Seignory or by the Senate, be obliged to assemble the Prerogative Tribe, or representative of the people, in arms by sound of trumpet, with drums beating and colors flying, in any town, field, or marketplace being not above six miles distant, upon the day and at the hour appointed, except the meeting through inconvenience of the weather or the like be prorogued by consent of the Seignory and the Tribunes; that the Prerogative Tribe being assembled accordingly, the Senate propose

to them by two or more of the Senatorian magistrates thereunto appointed at the first promulgation of the law; that the proposers for the Senate open to the people the occasion, motives, and reasons of the law to be proposed; and that the same being done, put it by distinct clauses to the ballot of the people. That if any material clause or clauses be rejected by the people, they be reviewed by the Senate, altered, and proposed, if they think fit, to the third time, but no oftener.

41. That what is thus proposed by the Senate and resolved by the people be the law of the land, and no other, except as in the case reserved to the Dictatorian Council.

42. That every magistracy, office, or election throughout this whole Commonwealth, whether annual or triennial, be understood of consequence to enjoin an interval or vacation equal to the term of the same. That the magistracy of a Knight and of a Burgess be in this relation understood as one and the same; and that this order regard only such elections as are national and domestic, and not such as are provincial or foreign.

43. That for an exception to this rule, where there is but one Elder of the Horse in one and the same Parish, that Elder be eligible in the same without interval; and where there be four Elders of the Horse or above in one and the same Parish, there be not under nor above half of them eligible at the same election.

44. That throughout all of the assemblies and councils of this Commonwealth, the quorum consist of one-half in the time of health, and of one-third part in a time of sickness, being so declared by the Senate.

II. For the Religious Part, it is proposed:

45. That the universities, being prudently reformed, be preserved in their rights and endowments for and towards the education and provision of an able ministry.

46. That the legal and ancient provision for the national ministry be so augmented that the meanest sort of livings or

benefices, without defalcation from the greater, be each improved to the revenue of one hundred pounds a year at the least.

47. That a benefice becoming void in any Parish, the Elders of the same may assemble and give notice to the vice-chancellor of either university, by certificate specifying the true value of that benefice; that the vice-chancellor upon a receipt of such certificate be obliged to call a congregation of the university; that the congregation of the university to this end assembled, having regard to the value of the benefice, make choice of a person fitted for the ministerial function and return him to the Parish so requiring; that the probationer, thus returned to a Parish by either of the universities, exercise the office and receive the benefits as minister of the Parish for the term of one year. That the term of one year expired, the Elders of the Parish assemble and put the election of the probationer to the ballot. That if the probationer have three parts in four of the balls or votes in the affirmative, he be thereby ordained and elected minister of that Parish, not afterwards to be degraded or removed but by the Censors of the Tribe, the Phylarch of the same, or the Council of Religion, in such cases as shall be to them reserved by act of Parliament. That in case the probationer come to fail of three parts in four at the ballot, he depart from that Parish; and if he returns to the university, it be without diminution of the former offices or preferments which he there enjoyed, or any prejudice to his future preferment; and that it be lawful in this case for any Parish to send so often to either university, and be the duty of either vice-chancellor, upon such certificates, to make return of different probationers, till such time as the Elders of that Parish have fitted themselves with a minister of their own choice and liking.

48. That the national religion be exercised according to a directory in that case, to be made and published by act of Parliament. That the national ministry be permitted to have no other public preferment or office in this Commonwealth. That a national minister, being convicted of ignorance or

scandal, be movable out of his benefice by the Censors of the Tribe, under appeal to the Phylarch or to the Council for Religion.

49. That no religion being contrary to or destructive of Christianity, nor the public exercise of any religion being grounded upon or incorporated into a foreign interest, be protected by or tolerated in this State. That all other religions, with the public exercise of the same, be both tolerated and protected by the Council of Religion; and that all professors of any such religion be equally capable of all elections, magistracies, preferments, and offices in this Commonwealth according to the orders of the same.

III. For the Military Part, it is proposed:

50. That annually, upon Wednesday next ensuing the last of December, the Youth of each Parish, under the inspection of the two Overseers of the same, assemble and elect the fifth man of their number, or one in five of them, to be for the term of that year Deputies of the Youth of that Parish.

51. That annually on Wednesday next ensuing the last of January the said Deputies of the respective Parishes meet in the capital of the Hundred, where there are games and prizes allotted for them, as has been shown elsewhere; [5] that there they elect to themselves out of their own number one Captain and one Ensign. And that of these games and this election, the magistrates and officers of the Hundred be presidents and judges for the impartial distribution of the prizes.

52. That annually, upon the Wednesday next ensuing the last of February, the Youth through the whole Tribe thus elected be received at the capital of the same by the Lieutenant, as commander in chief, by the Conductor, and by the Censors; that under inspection of these magistrates the said Youth be entertained with more splendid games, disciplined in a more military manner, and divided by lot into sundry parts or Essays, according to rules elsewhere given.

[5] *Oceana*, Order XXVI. See *Oceana* (Liljegren), pp. 210ff.

53. That the whole Youth of the Tribe thus assembled be the First Essay. That out of the First Essay there be cast by lot two hundred Horse and six hundred Foot; that they whom their friends will, or themselves can, mount be accounted Horse, the rest Foot. That these forces, amounting in the fifty Tribes to ten thousand Horse and thirty thousand Foot, be always ready to march at a week's warning; and that this be the Second Essay, or the standing army of the Commonwealth.

54. That for the holding of each province, the Commonwealth in the first year assign an army of the Youth consisting of seven thousand five hundred Foot and one thousand five hundred Horse. That for the perpetuation of these provincial armies, or Guards, there be annually, at the time and place mentioned, cast out of the First Essay of the Youth in each Tribe or Shire ten Horse and fifty Foot; that is, in all the Tribes five hundred Horse and two thousand five hundred Foot for Marpesia, the like for Panopea, and the like of both orders for the Sea-Guards, being each obliged to serve for the term of three years upon the State's pay.

55. That the Senate and the people, or the Dictator, having decreed or declared war, and the field officers being appointed by the Council of War, the General, by warrant issued to the Lieutenants of the Tribes, demand the Second Essay, or such part of it as is decreed, whether by way of levy or recruit. That by the same warrant he appoint his time and rendezvous; that the several Conductors of the Tribes or Shires deliver him the forces demanded at the time and place appointed. That a General thus marching out with the standing army, a new army be elected out of the First Essay as formerly, and a new General be elected by the Senate; that so always there be a General sitting, and a standing army, what Generals soever be marching. And that in case of invasion, the bands of the Elders be obliged to like duty with those of the Youth.

56. That an only son be discharged of these duties without prejudice. That of two brothers, there be but one admitted to foreign service at one time. That of more brothers

not above half. That whoever otherwise refuses his lot, except upon cause shown he be dispensed withal by the Phylarch, or upon penitence he be by them pardoned and restored by such refusal, be incapable of electing or being elected in this Commonwealth, as also, that he pay to the State a fifth of his revenue for protection, besides taxes. That divines, physicians, and lawyers, as also the trades not at leisure for the Essays, be so far forth exempted from this rule that they be still capable of all preferments in their respective professions with indemnity.

57. That upon warrants issued forth by the General for recruits or levies, there be an assembly of the Phylarch in each Tribe; that such volunteers or men being above thirty years of age as are desirous of further employment in arms, appear before the Phylarch so assembled; that any number of these not exceeding one moiety [6] of the recruits or levies of that Tribe or Shire may be taken on by the Phylarch, so many of the Youth being at the discretion of this Council disbanded as are taken on of the volunteers. That the levies thus made be conducted by the Conductor of the respective Tribe or Shire to the rendezvous appointed; and that the service of these be without other term or vacation than at the discretion of the Senate and the people, or such instructions to the General as shall by them in that case be provided.

IV. For the Provincial Part, it is proposed:

58. That upon expiration of magistracy in the Senate, or at the annual recess of one-third part of the same, there be elected by the Senate, out of the part receding, into each provincial Council four Knights for the term of three years, thereby to render each provincial Council, presuming it in the beginning to have been constituted of twelve Knights, divided after the manner of the Senate, by three several lists or elections of annual, triennial, and perpetual revolution or rotation.

[6] One-half.

59. That out of the same third part of the Senate annually receding there be to each province one Knight elected for the term of one year. That the Knight so elected be the provincial Archon, General, or Governor. That a provincial Archon, Governor, or General receive annually in April, at his rendezvous appointed, the Youth or recruits elected in the precedent month to that end by the Tribes, and by their Conductors delivered accordingly. That he repair with the said Youth and recruits to his respective province, and there dismiss that part of the provincial Guard or army whose triennial term is expired. That each provincial Governor have the conduct of affairs of war and of state in his respective province, with the advice of the provincial Council, and that he be President of the same.

60. That each provincial Council elect three weekly Proposers or Provosts after the manner and to the ends already shown in the constitution of Senatorian Councils; and that the Provost of the senior list during his term be President of the Council in absence of the provincial Archon or General.

61. That each provincial Council proceed according to instructions received from the Council of State, and keep intelligence with the same, by any two of their Provosts, for the government of the province as to matter of war or of state. That upon levies of native, or proper arms, by the Senate and the people, a provincial Council, having to that end received orders, make levies of provincial Auxiliaries accordingly. That Auxiliary arms upon no occasion whatsoever exceed the proper or native arms in number. That for the rest, the provincial Council maintain the provincials, defraying their peculiar Guards and Council, by such known proportion of tributes as on them shall be set by the Senate and the people in their proper rights, laws, liberties, and immunities, so far forth as, upon the merits of the cause whereupon they were subdued, it seemed good to the Senate and the people to confirm them. And that it be lawful for the provincials to appeal from their provincial magistrates, councils, or generals to the people of Oceana.